THE ILLUSTRATED NATURAL HISTORY OF CANAD

The St. Lawrence Valley
KEN LEFOLII

Scientific consultants to the series: WALTER TOVELL, PhD, Director, Royal Ontario Museum; J. MURRAY SPEIRS, PhD, Department of Zoology, University of Toronto

Library of Congress Catalog Card Number: 72-109046

ISBN 0-9196-4404-X

N.S.L. Natural Science of Canada Limited
58 Northline Road, Toronto, Ontario M4B 3E5 Canada

Publisher: Jack McClelland
Editor-in-Chief: Peter Crabtree
Senior Editor: Michael Worek
Art Director: Peter Moulding
Visual Editor: Bill Brooks

Editorial Consultant: Pierre Berton

THE ST. LAWRENCE VALLEY

Art Director: Bill Fox
Artists: Vlasta van Kampen/Jerry Kozoriz
Gordon McLean/Huntley Brown/Gus Fantuz

Contents

Prologue

THE DESERT RIVER

The author visiting the St. Lawrence Seaway.

The Saint Lawrence is a desert river. The Saint Lawrence Valley lies between two high stone plains with both the qualities that define a desert: "an uncultivated wilderness with few inhabitants." Both stone plains are well watered and green in most seasons, but for human purposes they are deserts nonetheless. The Precambrian Shield north of the Saint Lawrence has about the same number of people, mile for mile, as the Sahara, and about as many pockets of fertile soil as there are oases in the desert sand. South of the Saint Lawrence the Appalachian Plateau is only marginally more hospitable.

Without the Saint Lawrence, this entire northeast quadrant of the continent would be a desert more formidable in some ways than the Sahara. Herodotus described Egypt as "the gift of the river." Canada is the gift of the Saint Lawrence.

The size of the gift is what makes the Saint Lawrence a great river, not the size of the watercourse. Measured against the other great rivers of the world, the Saint Lawrence is modest enough. Less than eight hundred miles from Lake Ontario, the Saint Lawrence reaches the sea. But the Amazon and the Nile run four thousand miles to the sea, the Mississippi, the Yangtze and the Congo more than three thousand. The Ob, in Western Siberia, is wider, deeper, and three times longer than the Saint Lawrence.

The greatness of the Saint Lawrence lies in the passage it opens to the continental interior and the new range of life the river introduces between the stone deserts on either side.

The nature of the Saint Lawrence is to animate a desert; to open a clear passage for a full spectrum of temperate-zone life forms that would otherwise hardly have migrated to this quadrant of the continent, or have survived here if they had; and to nourish all these forms of life once they had arrived. Geologically the Valley is a major frontier, the clash zone between two of the three great mountain systems that form the skeleton of North America. Biologically the Valley is again a major frontier, but a friendly one that includes rather than excludes forms of life which elsewhere seek separate environments. The Saint Lawrence is the southern limit of most northern species, and the northern limit of many southern ones. Somewhere along or in the river there are probably representatives of more than half the Eastern North American flora and fauna, most of them flourishing. We are not the only migrant species to like it here.

To nourish this range of life at this pitch of fertility, the Saint Lawrence crowds into its small area a remarkable variety of separate miniature environments, from ultrasaline submarine caverns to alpine meadows. What makes this diversity possible, though, is the division of the Saint Lawrence into three major environments—the distinct worlds of the high river, the valley, and the estuary.

The chapters that follow explore these worlds in turn, beginning here at the head of the Saint Lawrence, where the high river emerges from Lake Ontario.

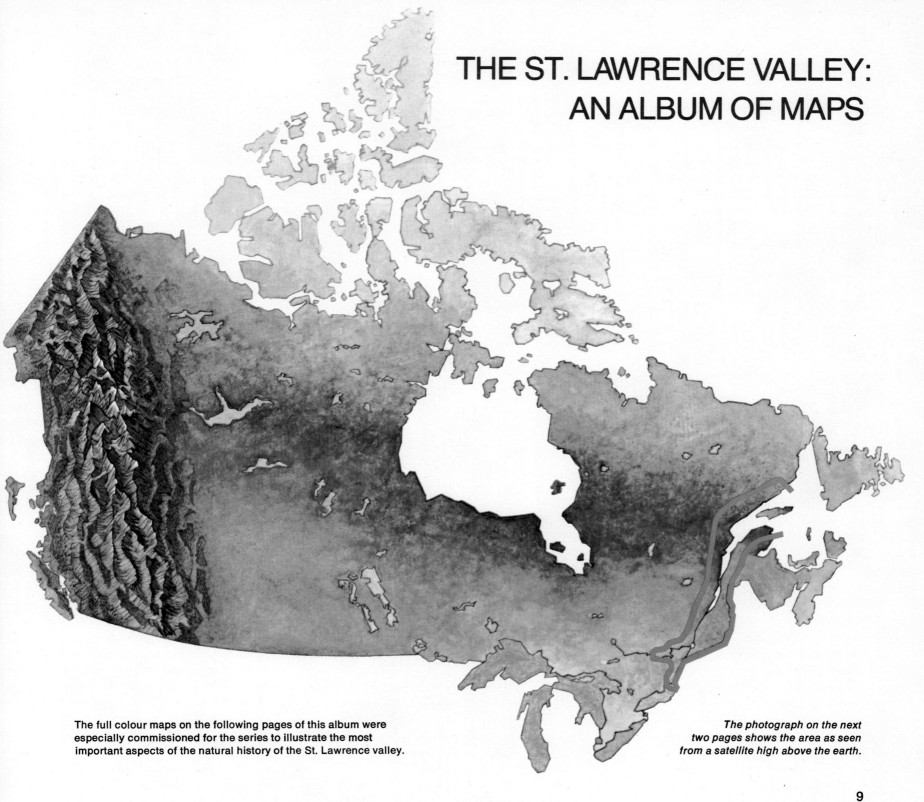

THE ST. LAWRENCE VALLEY:
AN ALBUM OF MAPS

The full colour maps on the following pages of this album were especially commissioned for the series to illustrate the most important aspects of the natural history of the St. Lawrence valley.

The photograph on the next two pages shows the area as seen from a satellite high above the earth.

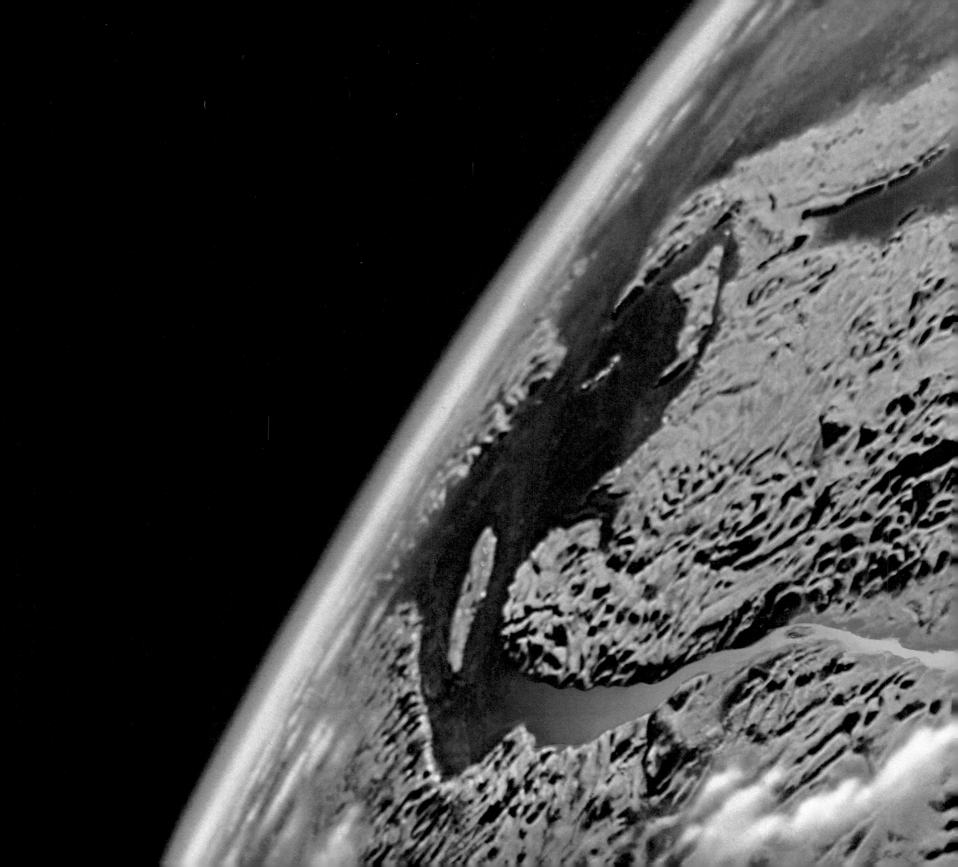

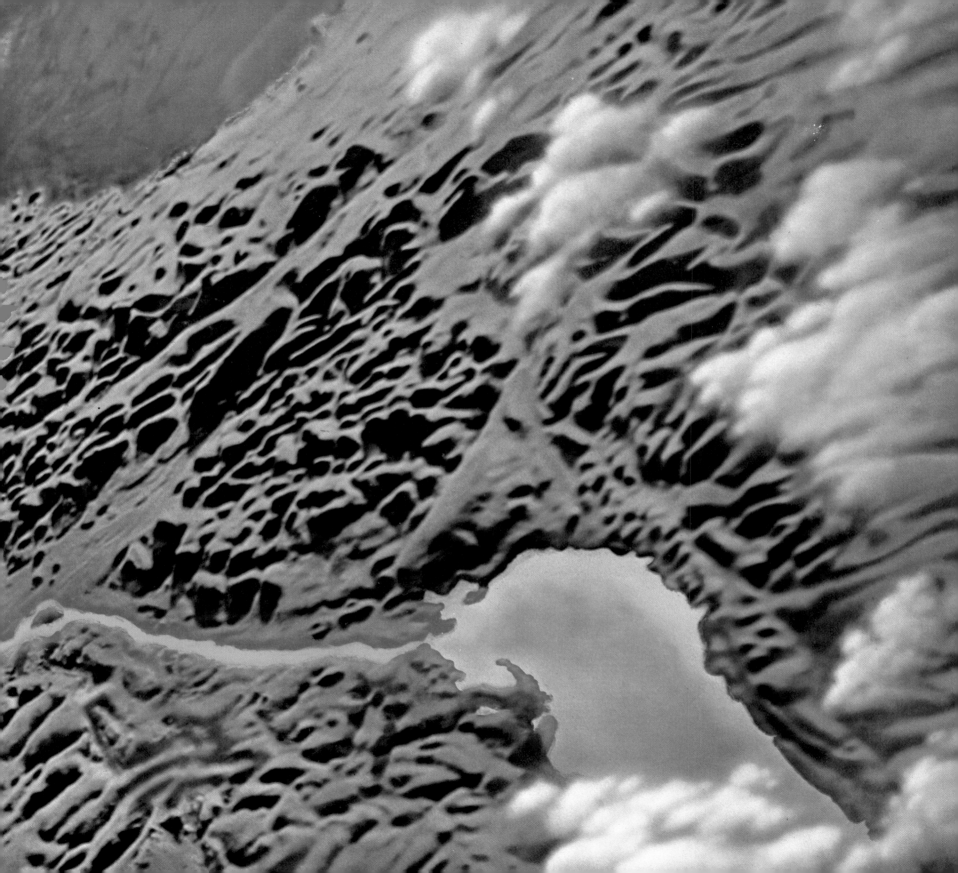

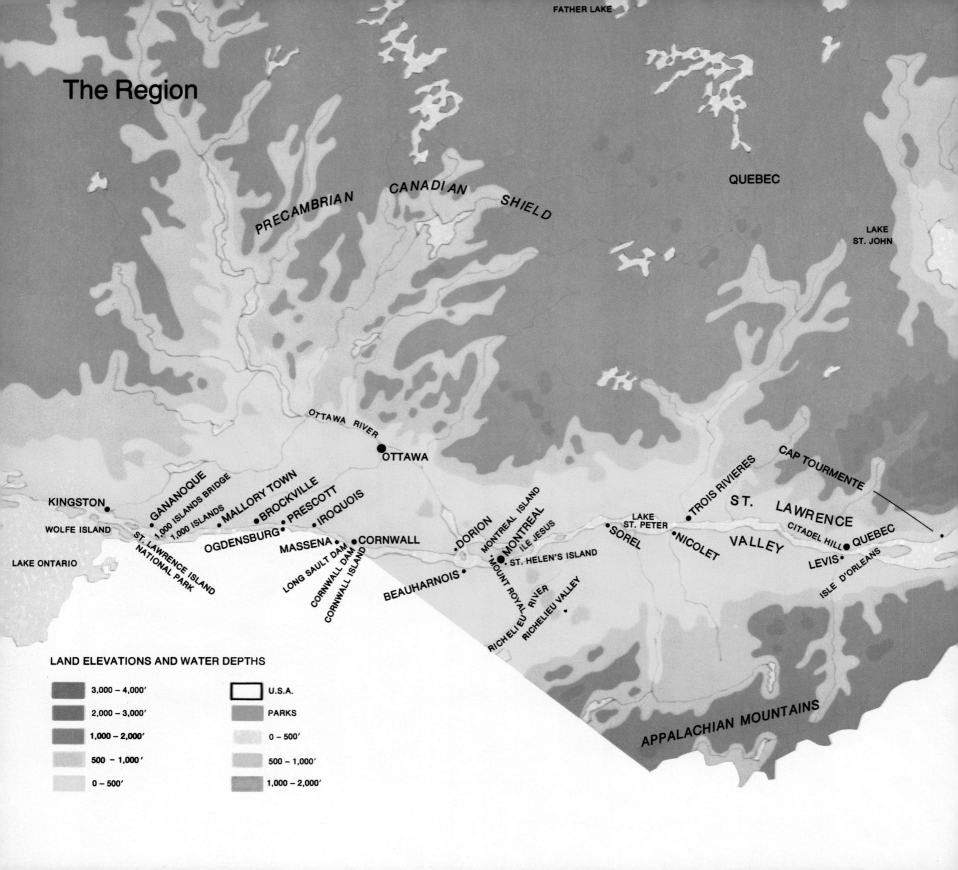

The Region

FATHER LAKE

PRECAMBRIAN   CANADIAN   SHIELD

QUEBEC

LAKE
ST. JOHN

OTTAWA   RIVER

● OTTAWA

CAP TOURMENTE

KINGSTON
●

GANANOQUE
1,000 ISLANDS BRIDGE
● 1,000 ISLANDS
● MALLORY TOWN
● BROCKVILLE
● PRESCOTT
● IROQUOIS

TROIS RIVIERES

ST.   LAWRENCE

WOLFE ISLAND

ST. LAWRENCE ISLAND
NATIONAL PARK

OGDENSBURG
●

MASSENA
● ● CORNWALL

DORION

MONTREAL ISLAND
MONTREAL
ILE JESUS

LAKE
ST. PETER
●

NICOLET
●

CITADEL HILL
●

VALLEY

QUEBEC
●

LAKE ONTARIO

LONG SAULT DAM
CORNWALL DAM
CORNWALL ISLAND

BEAUHARNOIS
●

● ST. HELEN'S ISLAND
MOUNT ROYAL

SOREL
●

LEVIS
●

ISLE D'ORLEANS

RICHELIEU   RIVER
RICHELIEU VALLEY

APPALACHIAN MOUNTAINS

LAND ELEVATIONS AND WATER DEPTHS

3,000 – 4,000'	U.S.A.
2,000 – 3,000'	PARKS
1,000 – 2,000'	0 – 500'
500 – 1,000'	500 – 1,000'
0 – 500'	1,000 – 2,000'

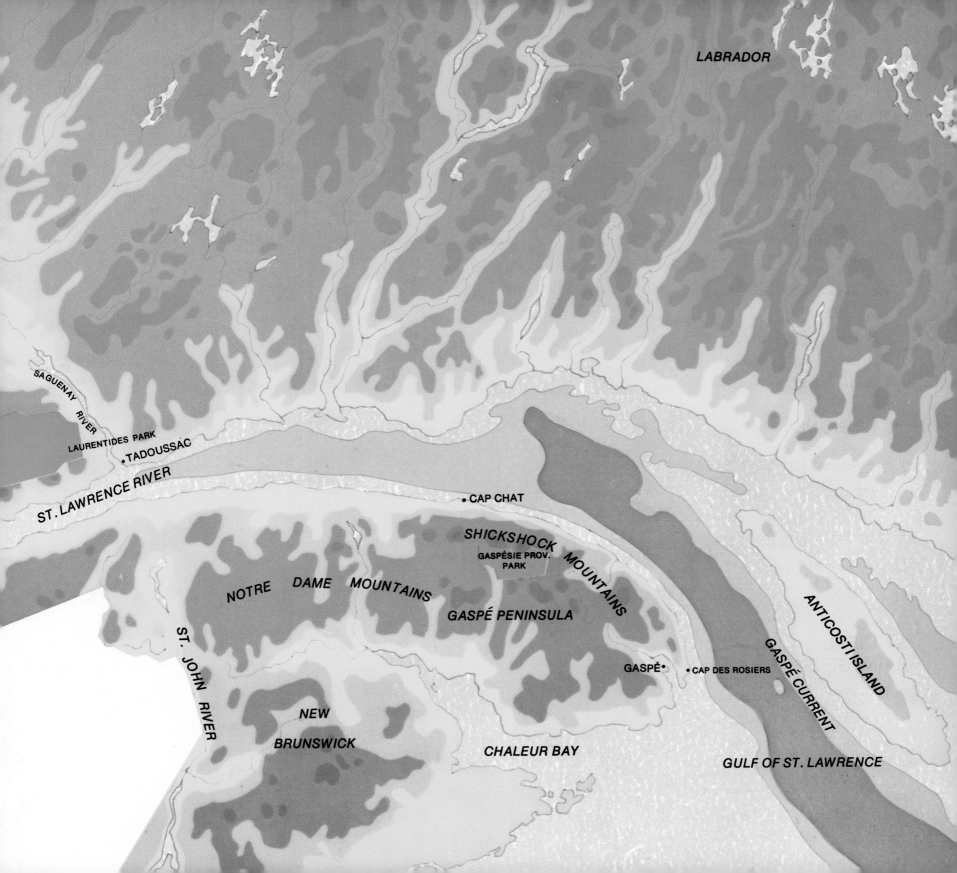

GEOLOGY

The St. Lawrence river connects Lake Ontario with the Atlantic Ocean. In its valley are a series of rocks, beginning with those of the Canadian shield, that reveal an important segment of Canadian geology. The map at the right indicates general rock types, which cover nearly 500 million years of geological history.

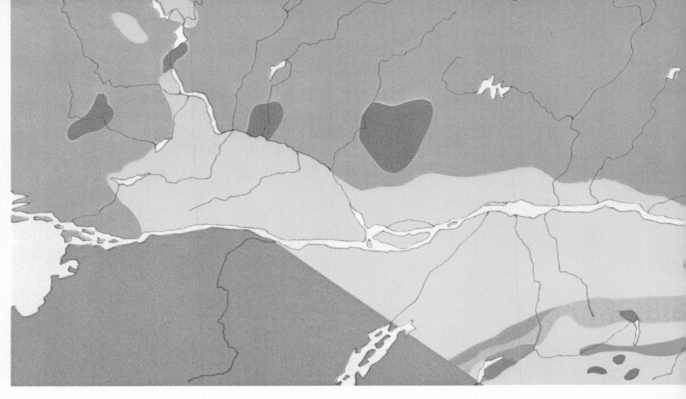

BASIC ROCKS	DEVONIAN
ACID ROCKS	SILURIAN
ORDOVICIAN	ACID, BASIC ULTRA BASIC ROCK
PALAEOZOIC	PERMIAN
CAMBRIAN	PROTEROZOIC

SOIL REGIONS

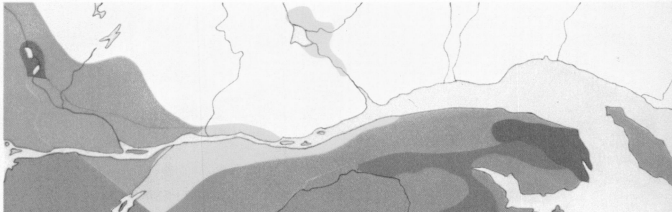

GREY WOODED SOILS	PODZOL SOILS WITH ROCK OUTCROPS, PEAT
BROWN PODZOL SOILS	BROWN PODZOLIC SOILS
DARK GREY GLEISOLIC SOIL	PODZOL SOILS
GLEISOLIC SOIL – BROWN FOREST SOIL	PODZOL SOILS WITH ROCK OUTCROPS
ROCK OUTCROPS	

PRINCIPAL DRAINAGE BASINS

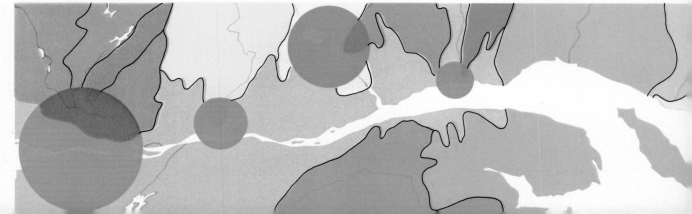

ST. LAWRENCE (OUTARDES)	BETSIAMITES
OTTAWA	MANICOUAGAN
GATINEAU	KOKSOAK
LIEVRE	ROMAINE
ST. MAURICE	ATLANTIC BASIN
SAGUENAY	ST. JOHN

PROPORTIONATE AVERAGE DRAINAGE

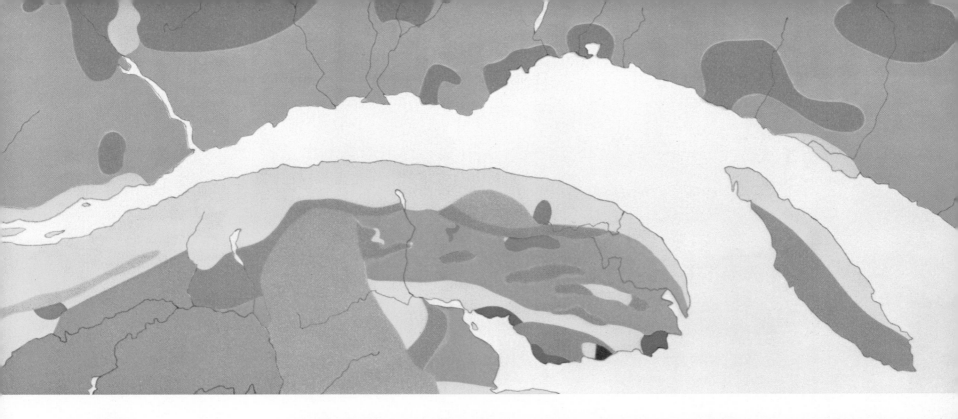

INLAND FISH

SMALL-MOUTH BLACK BASS	▲
NORTHERN PIKE	○
AMERICAN EEL	☆
WALLEYE	✳
BROOK TROUT	■
ARCTIC CHAR	▽
ATLANTIC SALMON	✳

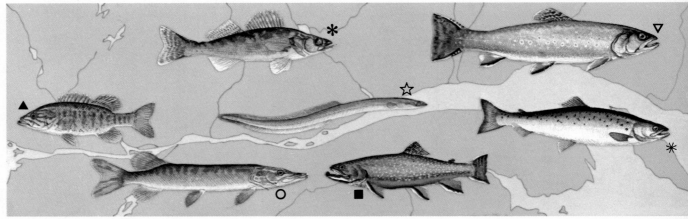

COMMON BIRDS

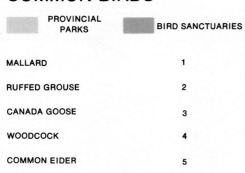

	PROVINCIAL PARKS		BIRD SANCTUARIES

MALLARD	1
RUFFED GROUSE	2
CANADA GOOSE	3
WOODCOCK	4
COMMON EIDER	5

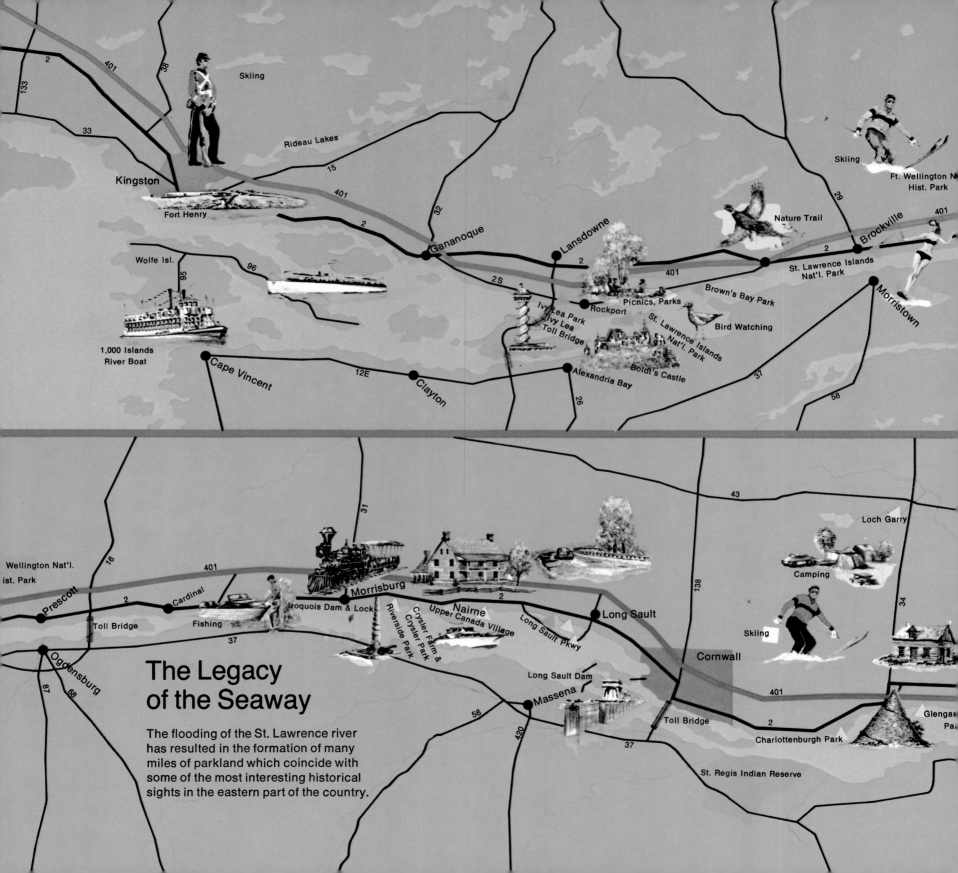

The Legacy of the Seaway

The flooding of the St. Lawrence river has resulted in the formation of many miles of parkland which coincide with some of the most interesting historical sights in the eastern part of the country.

Skiing

Rideau Lakes

Kingston

Fort Henry

Wolfe Isl.

1,000 Islands River Boat

Cape Vincent

Clayton

12E

Gananoque

Lansdowne

Rockport

Ivy Lea Park
Ivy Lea
Toll Bridge

St. Lawrence Islands Nat'l. Park

Boldt's Castle

Alexandria Bay

Picnics, Parks

Brown's Bay Park

Bird Watching

Nature Trail

St. Lawrence Islands Nat'l. Park

Brockville

Ft. Wellington N Hist. Park

Skiing

Morristown

Wellington Nat'l. ist. Park

Prescott

Ogdensburg

Toll Bridge

Cardinal

Fishing

Iroquois Dam & Lock

Morrisburg

Crysler Farm & Crysler Park
Riverside Park

Nairne

Upper Canada Village

Long Sault Pkwy

Long Sault Dam

Massena

St. Regis Indian Reserve

Long Sault

Cornwall

Toll Bridge

Charlottenburgh Park

Loch Garry

Camping

Skiing

Glenga Pa

PART ONE / THE REGION

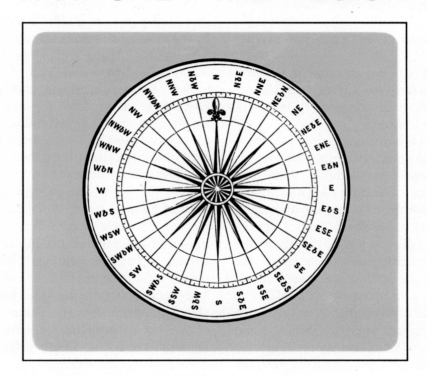

1 THE HIGH RIVER

The bowl that cups Lake Ontario rises steeply from depths of more than two hundred feet at the eastern end. Here, about ten miles apart, there are two gouges nicked from the rim of the bowl, neither much more than thirty feet deep or five hundred feet wide. For several miles the gouges run parallel courses east from the lake; then they meet in a rough, often divided trench that strikes northeast toward the Atlantic. Eight hundred miles beyond the lake and 243 feet below it, the trench, now seventy miles wide, finds the sea.

This is the Saint Lawrence River. We are about to follow it downstream, exploring its course from the surface, from the air, and sometimes from below, with the occasionally more interesting view that opens to the eye of a fish.

Water escaping from Lake Ontario runs through the twin gouges in the rim of the lake at about two knots. Big vessels plying the main shipping channel, the southerly of the two gouges, are subject to a speed limit. When they are moving upstream, the limit is nine knots; downstream they are allowed to add the speed of the current, and make eleven knots "over the bottom." This is a fairly sedate pace for a river the size of the Saint Lawrence, but for the first fifty miles of its course the riverbed is almost level; the run downhill comes later. Indeed, for the first thirty miles the river in a sense runs uphill. The gouges in the rim of Lake Ontario deepen slightly as they leave the lake, then become shallower as they approach the Thousand Islands Bridge at Ivy Lea, on the Canadian shore. From the main span of the bridge, suspended 150 feet above the river, the line of sight upstream encounters first a cluster of small islands that seem to clog the channel. These are outcrops of the highest point in the riverbed, the sill between Lake Ontario and the Saint Lawrence. Strictly speaking, the divided reach of water between the open lake and the sill might more accurately be called a bay of Lake Ontario. Beyond the sill, the river itself begins to descend, at first very slowly, toward the sea.

Looking out, again, from the main span of the suspension bridge, the line of sight in either direction hardly seems to follow a river at all. Rather, the locked and crossed arms of water among the protruding knobs of rock resemble some shallow Laurentian lake. These are the celebrated Thousand Islands. Their similarity to the Laurentian landscape is legitimate. Most of the rock is very old granite, rough to the touch and vaguely pink to the eye—Precambrian rock that here forms a low bridge between the Shield on the north and the Adirondack uplands on the south. The rock bridge, known to geologists as the Frontenac Axis, is less than fifty miles wide where the riverbed crosses it.

Crossing the Frontenac Axis by land, on Highway 2 northeast from Kingston, a reflective driver can easily be overtaken by the sense of a journey through time. The road dips and rises with the undulating rock along the riverbank. Almost every rise is capped by a thin layer of limestone, worn away in the hollows to the underlying granite. Inland seas flooding the Great Lakes basin from the south and the west built up the limestone several hundred million years ago; wind, water and ice stripped most of it away; but among the recurring limestone caps of the riverbank hills, the lapping of the old seas against the older granite seems to have left an echo.

On the water, the passage from limestone to granite is marked by the islands. Wolfe Island, the rise of land between the two channels gouged from the rim of the lake, has the smoothed contours of the old seabed; grey limestone banks curving upward to open fields. But as the channel approaches the sill of the river, the character of the islands changes abruptly. They jut steeply from the water, bare granite at the base, rugged above, stone dreadnaughts that match in some cases their memorable but nevertheless forgotten names: Bloodletter Island, Dumfounder Island, Deathdealer Island. Like ships, too, the granite islands are banded at the water line with a discoloured ring; it marks, in the case of the islands, the high and low stages of the river. The bank is little more than two feet deep, an indication of the remarkably constant flow of water from Lake Ontario—a predictable distinction, perhaps, for a river fed by a system of storage tanks on the scale of the Great Lakes.

Above the waterline pale green lichen dapples the pinkish granite, and above the lichen, trees grip all but the smallest rocks. They grow in unpredictable patterns: on some islands nothing but broadleaved hardwoods, chiefly oak and hickory; on others, hardwoods mixed with cedar, spruce or fir; and on others, the evergreens alone. Here and there on the islands stands a resinous pine that grows nowhere else in Canada. Pitch Pine Island is named after this tree, which dominates the island. Closer to the ground, the islands are usually mantled by brush; ebony-spleenwort, New Jersey tea, hairy bush clover and, nearer the river margins, flowering rush.

Both the islands and the riverbanks are pocked with reedy marshland that enriches the life of the river by attracting migratory flights of great Canada geese, and a dozen varieties of ducks. Double-crested cormorants nest among the islands in summer; so do several varieties of gulls and terns, including the caspian tern, far from home. Hawks and a few bald eagles hunt the upper air and, sometimes, short-eared owls the lower. Now and then, at dusk, a pair of black-crowned night herons or great blue herons will be outlined against the surface gloss of the water, poised long-legged and beautiful over the back eddies where small fish sometimes escape the current to rest.

Below the surface, carp have recently become so common that their gluttony is disrupting the food cycle, and eventually they will no doubt displace most of the other fish. But there are still perch in large numbers, pickerel, pike, some muskellunge and a few sturgeon browsing the riverbottom. The submarine terrain is a good deal rougher than anything suggested even by the harsh lines of the islands above the surface. The bottom plunges and rears wildly, all hard lines and jagged edges. With age a river smooths the underwater landscape; old river beds are streamlined. The Saint Lawrence, a very young river, is no less than thirty feet deep in the main shipping channel, but in many places drops over submarine cliffs to depths of 250 feet, then rises and falls again. This is an ideal world for many river fish. Shelter from the current is never far away, and near the shores are all the combinations of water movement and topography favoured by plankton, the small organisms most fish feed on.

Of the Thousand (or more) Islands, twelve widely scattered ones are still the common property of anybody who wants to visit them—The Saint Lawrence Islands National Park. The islands of the park can be reached only by boat. While there are no ferry routes among the islands, boats and guides are easy to hire in the riverside towns, particularly Gananoque. About fifteen miles downstream from Gananoque, just off Highway

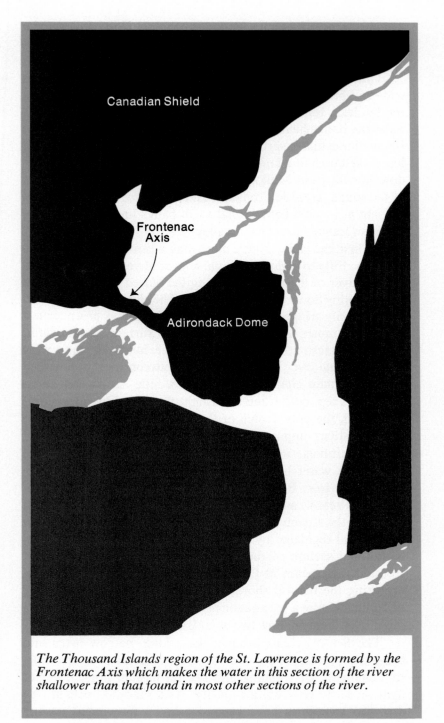

The Thousand Islands region of the St. Lawrence is formed by the Frontenac Axis which makes the water in this section of the river shallower than that found in most other sections of the river.

401, is the park headquarters on the mainland at Mallorytown Landing, where a naturalist will provide a more intimate description of the islands.

Offshore from Mallorytown Landing the river, five miles wide and broken by treed granite islands, still resembles a Laurentian lake. But here the stream begins to gather; within a few miles the banks have drawn within two miles of each other, the island clusters have shrunk in size and numbers, and the current has picked up half a knot of speed. At Brockville, thirteen miles downstream from Mallorytown Landing, the river breaks free of the rough, granitic Frontenac Axis. Clear of island outcrops, straight as a canal between flat earth banks lined with willows, the Saint Lawrence enters its valley.

At first, the valley is little more than a gentle hollow between low hills. Fifty to eighty feet high, a layer of yellowish clay overlying a layer of limestone overlying the buried granite, the hills roll smoothly down to the riverbanks. The slopes are open parkland, heavily fringed at the riverside with dense green waterweed in summer. A few feet below the surface of the water, banks of limestone no more than three hundred yards wide reach into the river from each side. Between these submerged banks the main channel, more than a mile across and about sixty feet deep, cuts a line so straight that the shipping route is unmarked, the only stretch of the river between Lake Ontario and the estuary unpunctuated by bells, buoys and flags.

The artificial appearance of the river here has natural causes; the water happens to find its lowest level in a ruler-straight line from Brockville to Prescott, ten miles downstream. Between Prescott and Cornwall, thirty-eight miles farther down the river, the stream regains a natural appearance but is in fact shaped and regulated by highly artificial means. This is the international section of the Saint Lawrence Seaway. Twice, at Iroquois, and again at Cornwall, huge dams block the river, drowning the natural shorelines including the original village of Iroquois, now a subaqueous ghost town. Where there was a rapid river there are now two quiet lakes.

The Seaway dams brought these long, narrow lakes into being during the 1950's. Among their consequences are wide, safe channels for shipping and several million horsepower of hydro-electric generating capacity. As a marginal benefit, the drowned shorelines have become heavily frequented nesting grounds for geese and ducks, among them blue-winged teal, mallards, pintails, black ducks and even a few relatively rare shovelers. Yet another consequence of the Seaway dams has been to convert into long reaches of calm water the rapids that once leaped down this stretch of the river. There were three: the Galops, Rapide Plat, and Long Sault. There could hardly have been a more vivid symbol of the Canadian experience than the rapids of the Saint Lawrence, and to learn that most of them are not merely bypassed, but obliterated, comes as an emotional wrench.

Unlike most landmarks, the rapids were less a spectacle than an experience—people looked at Niagara Falls, but they shot the rapids, imaginatively at least. Henry Beston, writing a book called *The St. Lawrence* in 1942, sounded as thrilled as any Victorian lady diarist: "A shudder, a strange motion downhill into a vast confusion and a vaster sound, and one is in the pool which is the climax of the rapids of the Long Sault. So steep is the winding rush downslope into the pool and out of it along a furious curve that the rims of water close along the banks stand higher than the tumult in the pit, and one passes, as it were, through banks of water as well as banks of land. Currents and agitations of wind, rapids of the invisible air, enclose the ship in a leap, scurrying the deck with their small and wild unrest. In the cauldrons all is giant and eternal din, a confusion and war and leaping-up of white water in every figure and fury of its elemental being, the violence roaring in a ceaseless and universal hue and cry of water in all its sounds and tongues. The forms of water rising and falling here, onrushing, bursting, and dissolving, have little kinship with waves at sea, with those long bodies of the ocean's pulse. They are shapes of violence and the instancy of creation, towering pyramids crested with a splash of white, rising only to topple upstream as the down-current rushes at their base. Lifted for an instant of being into a beauty of pure form and the rising curve . . ." and so on; but not any more.

Where the rapids were is now calm water. Local folk-history tells of one descent by canoe in fifteen minutes flat. At the foot of the Long Sault the canoe would have been driven by its thirty-six-mile-an-hour momentum well into a natural bulge in the river known as Lake Saint Francis. Spreading from either side of Lake Saint Francis lies the main basin of the Saint Lawrence Valley.

HIGHWAY FOR THE BIRDS

The St. Lawrence valley lowlands is a region heavy with marshes and damp underground, caused by water inundation from the St. Lawrence river during the construction of the seaway. This makes it a natural route for migrating birds. Conditions here are ideal for waterfowl; not only is there a vast profusion of prey, but the boggy environment also precludes human intrusion thus affording the birds suitable protection. The American coot (above) usually prefers to hide rather than flying off when threatened with danger.

The valley refuge

Although there is a predominance of aquatic birds in the St. Lawrence river valley the area also plays host to many land species like the woodcock and ruffed grouse. The birds have been one of the major beneficiaries of the seaway flooding. The river itself lies across several major bird flyways and large concentrations of birds stop at the river on their north-south migration each year to feed and rest.

► *A large pure white bird, with black wing tips, the snow goose passes through Cap Tourmente on its way to an Arctic nesting.*

The Canada goose, like the maple leaf, has become a national symbol.

The eider duck supports a small eider-down industry in the valley.

The male ruffed grouse fans its tail, struts and flutters up into overhead branches to attract the female in its mating display.

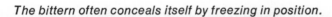

The bittern often conceals itself by freezing in position.

The woodcock is a nocturnal bird found in moist woodland

2 THE VALLEY

From the river, the floor of the Saint Lawrence Valley seems to be perfectly flat. This is a mild illusion. The bottom of the valley is concave, arching from the sides toward the river in a shallow curve. Close to the midpoint of the valley a ridge runs across the floor from the Precambrian Shield on the north to the Adirondack Dome on the south, subdividing the valley. Geologists, who call this ridge the Beauharnois Axis, speak of the basins on either side as two separate valleys, the Ottawa-Saint Lawrence Valley to the west, the Saint Lawrence Valley to the east. This book treats the region as one valley with two basins.

At ground level, the Beauharnois Axis that divides the valley is almost invisible. Like the Frontenac Axis near Lake Ontario, the Beauharnois Axis is a subterranean arch of Precambrian rock, longer but much lower and narrower. The arch in this case lies almost entirely hidden by a thick, relatively smooth mantle of sandstone. The underlying Precambrian rock of the arch breaks the surface only once, on the west shore of the Lake of Two Mountains, at the confluence of the Ottawa River and the Saint Lawrence. Here, between Dorion and Rigaud on Highway 17, the roadbed in a few places can be seen to cut through the granite of the Beauharnois Axis. Just west of the highway the granite breaks clear of the overburden altogether, and rises in a rough hillock called Rigaud Mountain.

Elsewhere in the valley the sandstone and limestone that cover the granite basement appear on the surface mainly in small outcrops. In most places the rock is covered by soil, glacial till or marine clay. The contours of the valley floor were rough-cut by glacial ice, then smoothed and trimmed by the movements of the Champlain Sea that once flooded both basins of the valley. The glacial soil is a hard grey paste lumpy with rock fragments, from gravel-sized pebbles to huge boulders. The marine clay, slightly darker to the eye but far lighter and finer to the touch, lies in large pockets above the glacial till.

Seen from the river, the valley appears to be a flat plain, but on the floor of the valley itself the flat claybeds can be seen to alternate with rolling outcrops of glacial till. The lines of the landscape are constantly broken by terraces left by the rise and fall of the Champlain Sea, and by sand or gravel deltas left by rivers that carried glacial meltwater from the highlands to the shifting margin of the sea. To an eye alive to the origins of these changes in the terrain, the sensation of traversing an old seabed can be remarkably vivid, even on a paved road. But from a height of land, say Rigaud Mountain, the character of the landscape shifts again, and it is the compact shape of the plain firmly cupped by the clear, hard lines of the mountain walls −the *valleyness* of the valley−that dominates the eye.

On the river, upstream from Cornwall, the full volume of the Saint Lawrence is controlled by a pair of dams that completely block the riverbed, the Cornwall Power Dam and the Long Sault Spillway Dam on the American side of the river. Below the dams, the flow of the river is pinched into two narrow channels on either side of Cornwall Island. Depending on how many of the power dam's sluiceways are open, the current forces its passage through the main channel, south of the island, at speeds between three and six knots. The water here is sometimes flecked with white−a pale afterimage of the drowned Long Sault Rapids. At the foot of the island the international boundary dips south, then strikes east along the forty-fifth parallel; from this point, the Saint Lawrence is entirely in Canada.

Below Cornwall Island the river opens abruptly into a long shallow reach four miles wide, called Lake Saint Francis, where the current slows again to less than two knots. Small, low islands stipple the lake, weeds and rushes fringe the shore, shadowed by scattered clumps of willow, elm and birch. The low clay banks are often drowned by rising water. Much of Lake Saint Francis is less than ten feet deep, with shoals and underwater banks that send dense growths of weed to the surface. In this softer underwater environment, slow-water fish are more plentiful than they are upstream; small and large-mouth bass, for instance, and Lancaster perch. Since the dams upstream began to regulate the flow of the river, making Lake Saint Francis even more sluggish than before, grass pike seem to have multiplied. Local fishermen say the grass pike are polluting the river; the pikes' real crime is a healthy appetite for young Lancaster perch, which the fishermen greatly prefer to pike.

The downstream end of Lake Saint Francis, twenty-seven miles beyond Cornwall Island, is blocked by a larger island, de Salaberry. Here again, the Saint Lawrence has been converted into an artificial watercourse. Originally, the river struck north of the island, dropping steeply and angrily through two more of its celebrated rapids, the Coteau and the Cedars. In time these rapids were bypassed, first by a canal on the south shore near the river, called the Beauharnois Canal, then by a bigger canal on the north shore, the Soulanges Canal. Now both are abandoned; a new trough as wide and deep as many sections of the river itself, the second Beauharnois Canal, loops several miles south through the valley. In the former main channel of the river, a network of dams and dykes diverts all but a trickle of the river's flow to the new canal; through the old rapids, the water barely moves at all.

The second Beauharnois Canal is now the main channel of the Saint Lawrence, fifteen miles long, up to half a mile wide, thirty feet deep, plugged at the foot by another great power dam. The Canadian and American power plants at Cornwall and the Canadian plant at Beauharnois are capable of generating almost five million horsepower of electrical energy. The exploitation of the Saint Lawrence's power is unusual for its thoroughness; the dams suck from the river almost all the power that's in it. Alongside the west wall of the Beauharnois dam a pair of locks drop seabound ships eighty-four feet to the juncture of the Ottawa and Saint Lawrence Rivers.

The Ottawa joins the Saint Lawrence in two arms. The main branch runs into the Saint Lawrence at Beauharnois to form a bulge in the river called Lake Saint Louis. But a few miles upstream a second arm of the Ottawa branches to the northeast, at first in a wide embayment known as the Lake of Two Mountains, then in two narrower channels that converge and join the Saint Lawrence about fifty miles downstream from Beauharnois. The northerly arms of the Ottawa and the main channel of the Saint Lawrence carve out among them a number of big islands: Ile Perot, Ile Bizard, Ile Jesus, and Montreal.

At Montreal the river has reached the heart of its valley and the height of its strength. Between Lake Ontario and Beauharnois an average of 230,000 cubic feet of water flows down the river every second. In the same second the Ottawa, after following a lower course through the clay and till beds of the valley, adds 70,000 cubic feet of darker, silted water. The river usually reaches its greatest rate of flow in May, slacks off to a low stage in September, rises slightly during the months of hard freeze, then rises sharply again during the spring breakup. At Three Rivers, where this seasonal variation has the most marked effect on the water line, the river surface rises five feet between September and May.

The actual amount of water passing Three Rivers in September is about half the amount that runs down the river in May. This seems a dramatic fluctuation at first glace, but the Ottawa carries twelve times more water in the spring than in the fall, the Columbia thirty-three times as much, and in a floodwater river like the Nile the variation is from a trickle to a deluge, making ratios of comparison meaningless. With a maximum flow only twice its minimum, the Saint Lawrence is among the most constant rivers in the world.

Toward the foot of Lake Saint Louis the low shores of the mainland and Montreal Island converge to shoot the current down the Lachine Rapids, the most storied of all the fast water reaches on the Saint Lawrence. This is where Champlain almost drowned learning to handle a canoe in white water, where La Salle plotted the epic voyages that never quite reached the Vermillion Sea and China, where des Ormeaux and his twenty-seven companions launched the raid on the Iroquois that ended in their own massacre on the Long Sault of the Ottawa.

The Lachine Rapids are still there, alone among the rapids of the Saint Lawrence. Foam still rides the dark water down the forty-five foot drop to Montreal harbour, although boats do not. In 1700 the masters of the fur trade dug a canal around part of the Lachine Rapids a foot and a half deep. That was just enough water to float a freight canoe. After this, Canadians seldom stopped digging on one shore or the other until the broad, placid canals and big locks of the Seaway's first leg were finished in 1959.

On either side of the river at Montreal, the landscape is deeply engraved by the special marks of the region's geological history; in their variety and frequency, the visible signs left by the events that shaped the terrain often overlap. St. Catherine's, the main eastward-trending street of Montreal, follows the beach of an inland sea that withdrew several hundred million

Almost alone, the Lachine Rapids have survived the building of the seaway, although the old river steamers have not been as successful.

years ago. The beach is now stone, covered by a thick mantle of clay deposited by the Champlain Sea not much more than ten thousand years ago. On this clay the pavement of St. Catherine's street was laid. But the cross streets of the city's east end run downhill from St. Catherine's on a bluff cut by the Saint Lawrence within the last two thousand years, during a high-water stage when the riverbed washed over much of what is now Montreal Island's downstream end.

Above St. Catherine's street the stone core of the island, Mount Royal, is itself a highly visible record of a geological curiosity, the eruption of seven volcanic blisters on the floor of the Saint Lawrence Valley long after all mountain-building activity in the northeastern quadrant of the continent had been over for a hundred million years. Mount Royal is the most westerly of these near-volcanoes. From here the others make an irregular arc across the valley toward the southeast.

On the northern horizon, the scarp of the Shield falls a thousand feet. This is the valley's northern wall, blue in most lights from a distance. Just south of the escarpment, and slightly to the west of north, lies a long gravel ridge overgrown by a mixture of broadleaved trees and evergreens; the gravel is glacial till,

the ridge a moraine built by the last glacier to withdraw from the valley. Farther south and east, a long dense line of mixed trees marks the frontier between a wide belt of sand and gravel terraces, once the successive beaches of the Champlain Sea, and a lower bed of clay where the Saint Lawrence flooded the plain when it was still swollen by the runoff from the melting glaciers.

To the south, the horizon is split. From the west, the Adirondack wall of the valley curves away into the valley of the Richelieu. Beyond the Richelieu the horizon rises again in a series of low folds known as the Sutton Hills—the outlying ridges of the Appalachian ranges that form the southern wall of the Saint Lawrence Valley between the Richelieu and the sea. The Richelieu rises in Lake Champlain, forty-six miles south of the Saint Lawrence, and runs almost due north in the cleft between the Adirondacks and the Appalachians until it spills onto the floor of the Saint Lawrence Valley, here so flat that the line of elms, willows and poplars along the banks of the Richelieu is a conspicuous landmark most of the way to the junction with the Saint Lawrence.

At about the midpoint of its passage across the valley floor

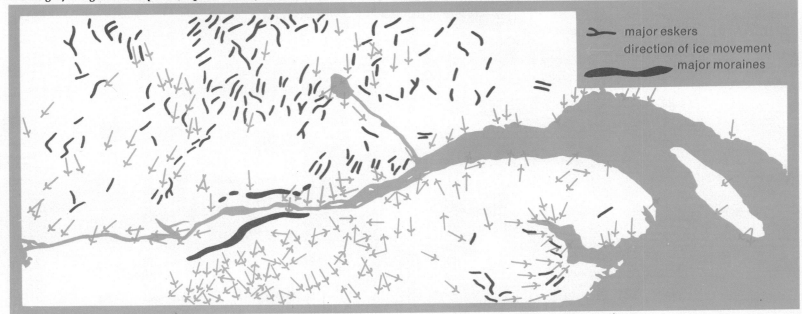

The direction of ice flow in the vicinity of the St. Lawrence valley was complex during the advances of the continental glaciers. The final melting of the glaciers deposited quantities of sand and rocks as their margins retreated northward, leaving behind moraines and eskers.

major eskers
direction of ice movement
major moraines

the Richelieu crosses a clay bluff that veers off to the west. The bluff is an old shoreline carved in the clay by Lake Montreal, the name given a former bulge in the Saint Lawrence during a stage of particularly high water. North of the old shoreline the Richelieu flows sluggishly across the plain, populated mainly by slow-water fish like walleye, bass and perch. The riverbed is mainly clay, but as it approaches the Saint Lawrence, on a line of sight a little north of each from the lookout on Mount Royal, it passes between two large stands of mixed forest, rising like islands from the flat clay plain.

They are, in fact, islands—island terraces of sand and gravel, sorted out by the shifting patterns of freshwater flow after the Champlain Sea had coated the valley floor with clay.

When the Saint Lawrence reaches the basin of Montreal harbour, the river is usually said to have descended to sea level. The actual case is less simple, since the level of the river rises and falls from season to season, the level of the sea from tide to tide and from season to season. The water levels mentioned in this book, like the ones commonly given for, say, the surface levels of the Great Lakes, are based on a statistical convention. The Canadian Hydrographic Service maintains fixed water-level gauges at thirty-four points along the river, with the primary gauge at Father Point, on the south shore of the Saint Lawrence estuary. From the readings at Father Point, hydrographers calculated the mean water level there for the years between 1941 and 1956. This mean level was then accepted, by agreement between Canadian and American mapmakers, as the "standard reference zero," or absolute sea level, so to speak, for elevations on the Saint Lawrence and the Great Lakes. Measured by this kind of arithmetic, the surface of Montreal harbour is reported to be eighteen feet above sea level, while the surface at Father Point is reported to be seven and a half feet below sea level. For practical purposes, though, the Saint Lawrence below Montreal no longer drops; it follows a level course toward the sea.

On the water, the distance from Montreal to the harbour at Quebec City is 138 nautical miles, most of the way between fairly low clay banks. At Sorel the river widens for fourteen miles to form Lake Saint Peter, a shallow, slow-moving reach of water more than seven miles across at its widest point. A miniature archipelago of low, mud-banked islands clogs the entrance to the lake, and the shores fall away in broad, reedy

Between Toronto and Montreal the St. Lawrence drops 250 feet. Ships are able to traverse the river only because of the seven seaway locks.

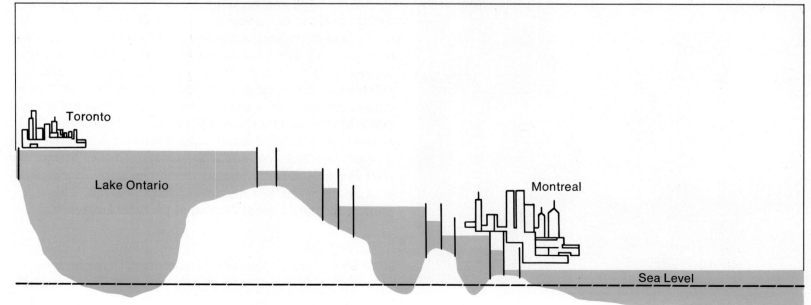

marshes that are a sanctuary for large colonies of sea birds, ducks, bustards and snipes. Below the lake the Saint Lawrence cuts a fairly regular channel, an average of two and a third miles wide, to within a few miles from Quebec City. Here the walls of the valley converge and, finally, pinch the Saint Lawrence Lowlands to an end.

Between Montreal and Quebec the river's course has taken it barely two degrees north, but this is the margin of passage between the soft-edged, relatively temperate world of the valley and the hard sub-arctic environment of the stone deserts to the north and east. At Montreal the average daily mean temperature reaches a high of fifty-one degrees and a low of thirty-six; at Quebec, the high is forty-eight degrees and the low is thirty-three. One result is a significantly longer growing season at Montreal: an average of 172 frost-free days in the year, compared to 147 days free of frost at Quebec. "The wind and weather of Montreal are often entirely different from what they are at Quebec," wrote Peter Kalm, a Swedish naturalist who sojourned on the Saint Lawrence in 1747. "Several sorts of fine pears will grow near Montreal, but are far from succeeding at Quebec, where the frost frequently kills them. Quebec has generally more rainy weather, spring begins later and winter sooner than at Montreal, where all sorts of fruits ripen a week or two earlier than at Quebec."

Ice, forming and breaking on the river, can be read as a natural guide to the increasing severity of the climate between the heart of the valley and the sea. Below Montreal, a firm ledge of ice running like a false shore from either bank of the river has usually formed by the end of December. Below Quebec, the shorefast ice forms early in December, and the ice ledges along either bank are both wider and thicker—the amount of ice that rides the current past Quebec is no more than one-fiftieth the amount that passes the mouth of the Saguenay, a hundred miles downstream. But here at the Saguenay ice never bridges the river completely, partly because the current is too strong, partly because the water is a mixture of fresh and salt. This is the estuary, the third natural division of the Saint Lawrence.

Montmorency Falls, a popular attraction, drop 250 feet from a former arm of the St. Lawrence over the edge of the Canadian shield.

3 THE ESTUARY

Although the Saint Lawrence meets the Precambrian Shield near Quebec, the great rock of Quebec—Citadel Hill—is not the rock of the Shield. Rather, Quebec stands on a tilted block of dark grey shale banded by thin, broken arcs of white calcite. This is sedimentary rock, several hundred million years younger than the predominantly granite Shield. From the riverbank the rock of Quebec rises in a sheer face 340 feet high, then slopes away to a narrow valley on the other side. In the middle distance the valley ends against a steep, heavy wall, the scarp of the Shield. The valley itself was once an arm of the Saint Lawrence; the rock of Quebec then stood in the middle of the river, as the island of Montreal does now. But the arm of the river that encircled Quebec was fairly short. Five miles downstream the scarp of the Shield comes within half a mile of the present Saint Lawrence channel. Here, where the abandoned arm of the river rejoined the main stream, the Montmorency River spills over the edge of the Shield and falls 250 feet to a basin worn in the shale below. (At Niagara the water drops 150 feet.)

Between Quebec and the mouth of the Montmorency River, the shoreline of the Saint Lawrence shifts with the water level. When the river is high, the stream follows a grassy clay bank. Low water uncovers a ledge of shale, up to a mile wide, thickly caked with mud. Like so many of the natural terraces along the course of the Saint Lawrence, the shale ledge was formed as the beach of an ancient sea. The ledge stretches, in broken sections, four hundred miles downstream from Quebec. Above the ledge, for most of this distance, a narrow riverside plain runs back a mile or two from the Saint Lawrence to the granite wall of the Shield. But often enough, to give the impression of locking the river in a vault of stone, the Shield thrusts all the way to the water's edge. Cap Tourmente, twenty-five miles below Quebec, is the first such headland of the Shield to emerge on the river. The crown of Cap Tourmente rises 1874 feet, and this, with local variations, is close to the average height of the stone plateau beyond the river.

Much the same pattern repeats itself on the opposite shore of the Saint Lawrence. Below Levis, the smaller port across the river from Quebec, the Appalachian range known as the Notre Dame Mountains presses toward the Saint Lawrence from the south. Unlike the steep granite face of the Shield, the limestone and shale folds of the Notre Dame Mountains unroll toward the river in a series of smoothed foothills, and in most places they leave a wider foreshore plain between the hills and the riverbank. But one of these smooth hills stands right in the middle of the stream: Isle d'Orleans, a rounded slate ridge thickly mantled with fine clay, eighteen miles long and almost five hundred feet high at the peak of the ridge.

Isle d'Orleans marks the seaward frontier of the mixed temperate forest that once covered the Saint Lawrence lowlands but survives only in isolated stands among the cleared fields. Cartier found wild grapes and cherries here, walnut and beech, maple and oak, along with the spruce and fir that dominate the riverbanks and the high ground on either side from about this point to the sea. On the north shore the trees of the mixed temperate forest reappear once, in the valley of the Saguenay leading inland to Lake Saint John. But this pocket of broad-leaved trees is an intrusion on a northern world of slow-growing, twisted evergreens, lichen, moss, and ground-hugging arctic weeds.

On the south shore the frontier between the temperate world and the northern one is less clearly marked. Scattered clumps of sugar maple, ash, and elm appear among the evergreens all the way from Isle d'Orleans to the sea. But although the frontier is indistinct, it is real; below Orleans, black and white spruce dominate the forest.

As the character of the land on either side changes, so does the nature of the river. Again, the downstream margin of Isle d'Orleans marks a frontier between two worlds. This is the tidal divide of the Saint Lawrence. Here the tidal rise of the river reaches its peak; here the penetration of salt water ends; here the brackish world of the estuary replaces the freshwater world of the river.

Between Isle d'Orleans and the Gulf of Saint Lawrence, the river channel opens gradually but regularly from a width of about seven miles at Cap Tourmente to more than seventy miles at Seven Islands. Seen from the crest of the tide as it advances from the Gulf, the river channel resembles a long stone funnel. Pouring into the funnel, the tidal water is lifted even higher

The influx of sea-water during high tide causes the flooding of many bays and inlets which drain almost completely dry during low tide.

by simple hydraulics, as the water forces a passage between the narrowing walls of the channel. Thus the level of the river rises about eight feet between low and high tide at Seven Islands, but rises almost sixteen feet at Isle d'Orleans. When the tidal crest passes Orleans its main strength is spent.

Waning speed is one measure of the tide's loss of strength as it penetrates the river. From Seven Islands the tidal crest thrusts 184 miles to Tadoussac, at the mouth of the Saguenay River, in about seventy minutes. From Tadoussac, the crest takes almost three hours to advance less than ninety miles to the tip of Isle d'Orleans.

The speed and height of the tidal flow remain almost constant from season to season. But this is not to say that the actual height and flow of the river conform to the mathematical precision of the tides. For one thing, the volume of water carried downstream by the river itself is much less regular here in the lower Saint Lawrence than it was in the upper reaches, where the enormity of the Great Lakes curbs seasonal fluctuations in the water level of the river. But the Ottawa discharges twelve times as much water into the Saint Lawrence in the spring as it does in the fall, as do the smaller tributaries between Montreal

and Quebec, so that in the narrows above Quebec the surface of the river is sometimes eight feet higher in May than it was in September. Moreover, strong winds blowing with or against the tide sometimes change the predicted level of the river by as much as three feet.

Within the moving body of the river, the thrust and retreat of the tides create patterns of flow infinitely more subtle than these surface observations suggest. The velocity of the tidal currents, for instance, changes with the depth of the water. Flow at the surface is relatively slow, but increases steadily to a depth of about twenty feet, where the surface water is moving at about two feet per second. Below twenty feet the velocity falls off, again in a steady curve, until at the bottom of the river the water is usually moving slightly slower than the water at the surface. For this reason, marine charts of the Saint Lawrence give the speed of tidal currents measured ten feet below the surface. Pilots can then make quick estimates of the average velocities on the hulls of the big ships.

From side to side, the tidal flow of the river varies even more widely than it does from top to bottom. Generally, the deeper and narrower the channel the stronger the current; but the con-

At the mouth of the Saguenay incoming tide forces cold water from the trough bottom upward into contact with the warm air, producing fog.

tours of the shores and riverbottom can change both the direction and speed of the tidal streams. At Crane Island, a few miles downstream from Isle d'Orleans, both the ebb and flood tides set parallel to the shoreline. The ebb flows at about three knots and the flood at two knots. But just ten miles down the river in the Saint Roche Traverse, a narrow channel flanked by shoals, the first rise of the flood stream sets from north to south almost directly across the trend of the river. The flood tide here reaches a speed of more than seven knots, the ebb eight knots. Close to the north shore there is a second channel in the same reach of the river, wider and deeper than the Saint Roche Traverse. Both the flood and the ebb streams, in this second channel, are almost two knots slower than the streams in the Traverse. Here the ebb sets north, hard against the high stone bank of the river, and rebounds in strong back-eddies that whirl along the rocks.

Farther downstream, as the river widens, the tidal streams move less rapidly but weave more intricate patterns. A branch of the flood stream enters the Saguenay, which becomes a second-generation tidal river, picking up the pulses of ebb and flood from the Saint Lawrence. Between low water and high, the Saguenay rises up to fourteen feet. On the ebb, this build-up of tidal water on the Saguenay discharges into the Saint Lawrence with great strength, setting up counter-currents half-way across the estuary.

At the juncture with the Saguenay, too, the main channel of the Saint Lawrence drops sharply to far greater depths—from between two and three hundred feet to a thousand feet and more. When the flood tide, advancing up this deep channel from the sea, strikes the steep underwater wall that rises to the shallower riverbed upstream, water from the deeper layers thrusts toward the surface. One result is low, heavy banks of summer fog, more frequent here than anywhere else on the Saint Lawrence. The fog condenses from moist air chilled by the upturning water of the deep channel. In midsummer, when the average surface temperature here is sixty degrees, the water between 150 and 300 feet down is sometimes half a degree colder than freezing point.

Salt, of course, accounts for the apparent contradiction of running water at ice-forming temperatures. Below the tidal divide at Isle d'Orleans, the fresh water of the upper river mixes with the salt water of the tidal flow. Above Orleans no salt water contributes to the tidal rise; the fresh water simply backs up, under pressure from the tidal inflow farther down the river. At the mouth of the Saguenay, the river is composed mainly of salt water. The fresh water from upstream, now mixed with sea-water, tends to flow in two streams that follow the shorelines, leaving the deep central channel to undiluted water from the sea.

But the salt water of this deep channel behaves differently from either the fresh water of the upper river or the salt water of the continental shelf. Fresh water reaches its greatest density at about forty degrees, which is why the Saint Lawrence (like all other streams and lakes) never freezes completely—ice forming on the surface insulates a layer of heavier, warmer water below. In the more complicated case of sea-water, temperature has less effect on density than salt content has, so that the saltiest water tends to sink regardless of its temperature. In the Gulf of Saint Lawrence, on the relatively shallow continental shelf, the water near the surface is warmer than the water below in summer, colder in winter, and less salty than the water below in both seasons. But in the deep channel of the Saint Lawrence something more interesting happens during the summer months. Below the warm surface layer of water, where the salt content is about twenty-nine parts per thousand, lies a second layer where the salinity goes up to thirty-two parts. In this zone the temperature is often less than thirty-two degrees even during July and August. Below this zone lies a third layer, where the salinity goes up to more than thirty-four parts per thousand, and the temperature goes up to forty-four degrees. During the winter this three-tiered structure breaks down. The two upper layers mix, and the temperature drops below freezing all the way from the surface to the warm, salty layer on the bottom. But the temperature of the bottom layer stays at forty-four degrees. At this depth the seasons change nothing.

The central channel of the Saint Lawrence, with its tiers of salt water, extends from the mouth of the Saguenay past the headlands of the Saint Lawrence and on across the floor of the Gulf to the rim of the continental shelf. Oceanographers' observations indicate that the deep waters of the Atlantic basin enter the channel at the rim of the shelf. Flowing mainly along the salty, relatively warm layer at the bottom of the channel, the Atlantic waters cross the floor of the Gulf into the Saint Lawrence river estuary.

Part of this oceanic stream reaches the mouth of the Saguenay, and wells up to cause the fogbanks mentioned earlier. Another part of the stream veers south across the Saint Lawrence well before it reaches the Saguenay, deflected by the shape of the north shore. The deflected part of the oceanic stream turns completely on itself by the time it stands off Cap Chat, on the south shore of the estuary, and from here it flows back to the sea.

The outflow of this oceanic stream along with the discharge of the upper Saint Lawrence forms a powerful, clearly defined stream known as the Gaspé Current. It runs parallel to the south shore, but stands about two miles out from the beach. From this margin to its midstream edge the Gaspé Current is usually about twelve miles wide, and for more than a hundred miles it flows downstream at about two knots during the ebb tide, slightly less during the flood. When the flood tide is advancing, the main flood stream passes the Gaspé Current to the north and a second, smaller flood stream passes between the landward side of the Current and the beach of the south shore. At these times, the estuary of the Saint Lawrence seems to be three rivers, the two flood streams flowing toward the continental interior while between them the Gaspé Current runs down to the sea.

Just where the river ends and the Gulf begins is a frontier unmarked by nature. The waters of the estuary are part of the general circulation of sea-water in the Gulf, and here at the mouth of the river the rich marine life of the estuary is not much different from the life of the Gulf. Geographically, the sharp southward curve of the Gaspé peninsula marks the end of the estuary on this shore, although the same slate and gray-wacke rocks follow the curve of the coast south from the rivermouth. On the north shore the same granite coastline continues its long sweep to the northeast.

Lacking a natural seaward frontier, the Saint Lawrence was given a statutory one by Royal Proclamation in 1763: a line extending from Cap des Rosiers, at the eastern end of the Gaspé Peninsula, to the West Point of Anticosti Island, and thence to the mouth of the Rivière St. Jean on the north shore abreast the western end of Anticosti Island. This imaginary line across almost ninety miles of tidewater, rather than the stone plains on either side, is the threshold of continental Canada.

A YOUNG RIVER
IN AN OLD VALLEY

This Pleistocene fossil is the remains of a fish which
once roamed the depths of the Champlain Sea. A legacy
of this extinct water mass, the fossil was found on one of
the ancient beaches which form an important part of the
present topography of the Saint Lawrence Valley.

The Adirondack dome

Two main features dominate the formation of our landscape – a continuous uplift of the land and the reverse process of surface erosion. When seas advance over land surfaces, sediments are deposited which eventually form new strata of sedimentary rock. These ancient, submerged strata are of major significance to the geologist in determining the age and formation of a region. Unconformities, which are time breaks between eroded surfaces and new strata, are especially significant in the Adirondack region where four types of rock assemblage can be distinguished. The oldest known sediments are referred to as the pre-Grenville complex, deposited about two billion years ago. One billion years ago, younger sedimentary rocks, the Grenville series, were laid down. After intense metamorphism, both these assemblages were eroded and the terrain flattened to form a surface over which the sea advanced about four hundred million

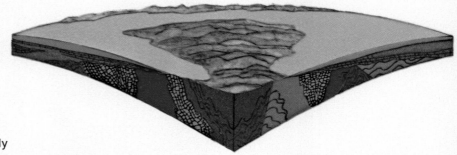

The Adirondack dome, shown here in the form of a peninsula, was connected to the Canadian shield and surrounded by the Palaeozoic sea. The dome underwent erosion from various natural forces and contributed sediment to the floor of these ancient seas.

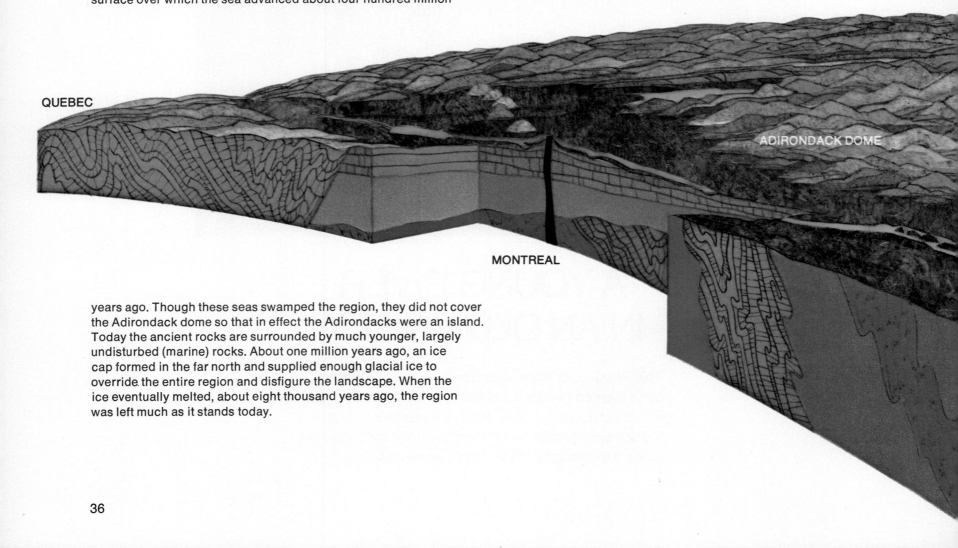

QUEBEC

ADIRONDACK DOME

MONTREAL

years ago. Though these seas swamped the region, they did not cover the Adirondack dome so that in effect the Adirondacks were an island. Today the ancient rocks are surrounded by much younger, largely undisturbed (marine) rocks. About one million years ago, an ice cap formed in the far north and supplied enough glacial ice to override the entire region and disfigure the landscape. When the ice eventually melted, about eight thousand years ago, the region was left much as it stands today.

36

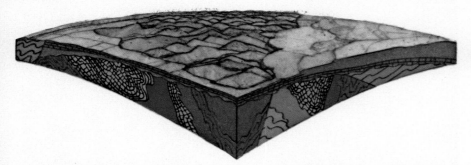

During the Palaeozoic era the Adirondack region, along with all of eastern North America, experienced uplifts from time to time, causing the seas to ebb and flow across the surrounding land. Erosion of the uplifted exposed land occurred during periods of sea withdrawal.

Four glacial advances and retreats have been recorded in North America. Here the glacial ice melts away for the last time from around the Adirondack region, depositing a mass of rock debris and sediments and exposing an altered landscape.

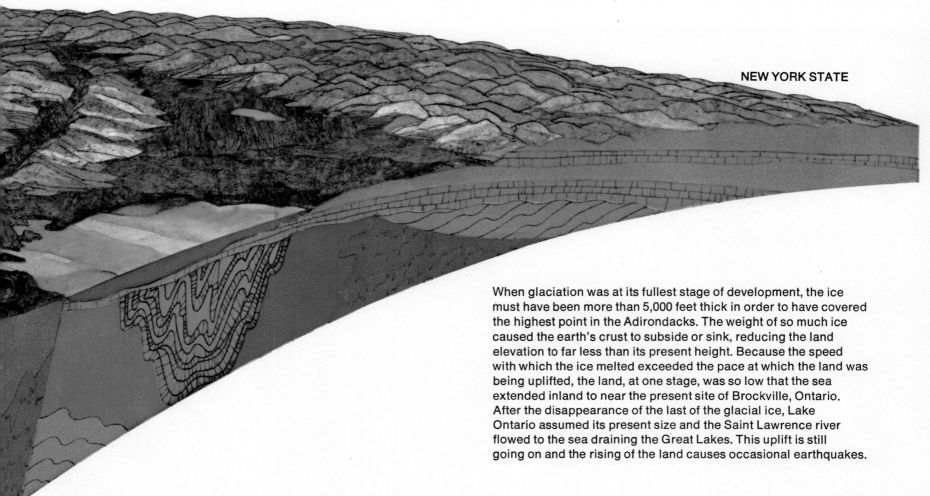

NEW YORK STATE

When glaciation was at its fullest stage of development, the ice must have been more than 5,000 feet thick in order to have covered the highest point in the Adirondacks. The weight of so much ice caused the earth's crust to subside or sink, reducing the land elevation to far less than its present height. Because the speed with which the ice melted exceeded the pace at which the land was being uplifted, the land, at one stage, was so low that the sea extended inland to near the present site of Brockville, Ontario. After the disappearance of the last of the glacial ice, Lake Ontario assumed its present size and the Saint Lawrence river flowed to the sea draining the Great Lakes. This uplift is still going on and the rising of the land causes occasional earthquakes.

Glaciers gouge a valley

The most striking feature of the morphology of the Saint Lawrence valley is the presence of a deep submarine trench, usually called the Laurentian channel, which extends from a point near the mouth of the Saguenay River to the edge of the continental shelf, a distance of about 750 miles, and frequently reaches a depth of over 1200 feet. Geological explorations have led to the theory that three major ice masses moved down the valley during the Pleistocene ice age; one mass originated from the valley of the Saguenay River, another advanced southward and was deflected eastward by the hard rock of Anticosti Island. The third major ice mass moved southward from the Labrador uplands, broadening and deepening the northern end of the Saint Lawrence submarine trough and creating a valley near the Strait of Belle Isle. The ice was thickest in the valleys causing exceptionally deep subglacial erosion of the valley beds.

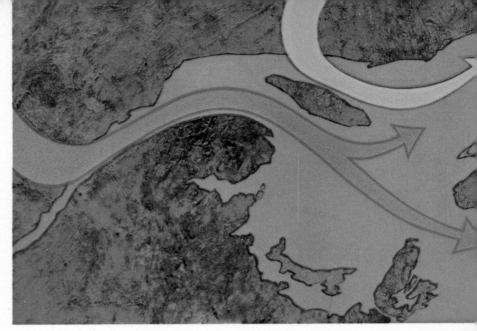

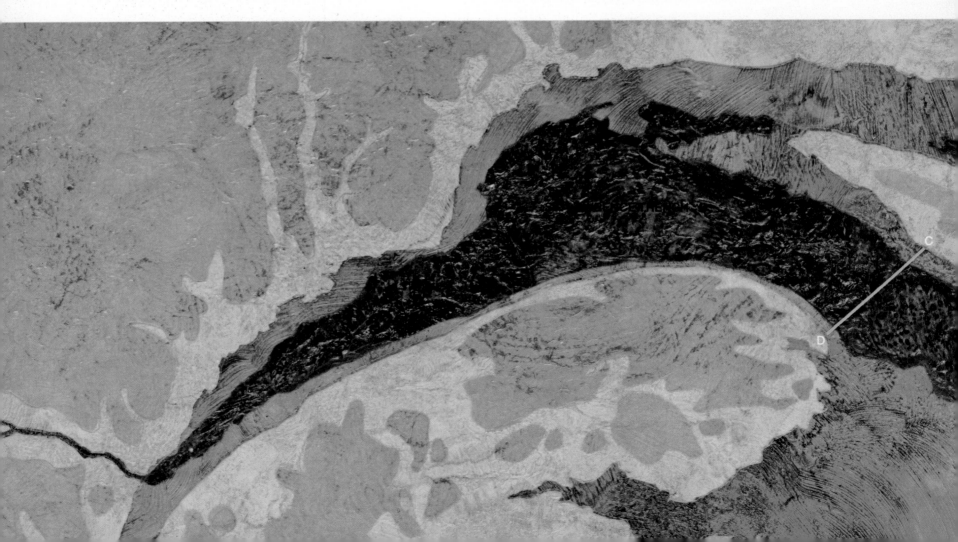

◄ Lobes of ice during the Pleistocene glaciation advanced southward from north of Anticosti Island and eastward from the mouth of the Saguenay River valley, slowly gouging out trenches that extend all the way to the edge of the continental shelf.

▼ If water was removed from the Saint Lawrence valley, the troughs shown in dark brown would be more than 900 feet deep. The two orange lines from Quebec to Anticosti Island and thence to the Gaspé peninsula indicate the location of the cross-sections (right).

◄ The seaward continuation of the Laurentian trough, extending completely across the continental shelf, is the natural extension of the preglacial St. Lawrence valley, modified through the effects of glacial erosion during the Pleistocene ice age.

▼ The cross-sections below show typical steep-sided submarine valleys, shaped primarily by glacial excavation. The broad base, relatively steep and straight walls and undulating profile are among the principal features of all such valleys.

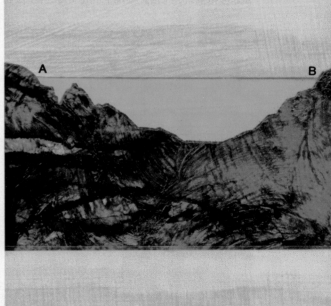

A sea invades the land

The earth's crust is very sensitive to changes in loads placed upon it. During the Pleistocene ice age the great weight of the ice depressed most of eastern Canada to such an extent that when the ice began to melt the sea invaded the Saint Lawrence and Ottawa valleys to well beyond the present city of Ottawa. The geological formation locally known as the "sand pits" represents the shore of the marine invasion of the Champlain Sea. The sea in turn vanished as the land slowly rose due to isostatic uplift after the melting of the ice. The most common marine sediments deposited by the invading sea was "leda clay" which is now being gradually eroded away. The white whale, or beluga, and the harbour porpoise are two of the mammalian species whose fossilized remains have been unearthed in Pleistocene deposits at several localities in the Saint Lawrence valley. Both these mammals are still relatively common today in the same areas in which they were found thousands of years ago.

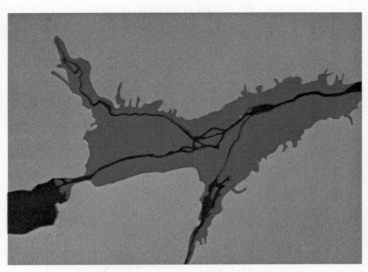

The inset map shows the gradual retreat of the Laurentian ice sheet and the extent of area of the emerging Champlain Sea.

Earthquake on the Saguenay

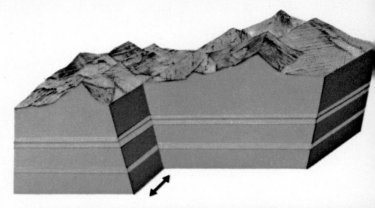

Current geologic thought views the earth's crust as a subterranean mass in constant motion and subjected to continual stresses which play an important role in the formation of mountains. The presence of the mountain, Cape Trinity (in the background of the pictorial scene opposite) was caused by volcanic intrusion near the mouth of the Saguenay River and is an extremely good indication that a deep trough, which parallels a rift or crack in the earth's crust, exists in this area of Quebec. One of the major effects of such geologic formations is the earthquake phenomenon. The picture itself depicts a French-Canadian family rushing from their home during the earthquake of February 1663 near the mouth of the Saguenay River. The landslide which occurred was doubtless triggered off by a quaking of the earth's crust, rendered almost inevitable by the thick deposits of marine clays laid down in the St. Lawrence and Ottawa watersheds which are peculiarly susceptible to any stirring within the earth's crust. The relative amount of damage which occurred during this earthquake equalled the complete devastation of San Francisco. Contemporary reports reveal a complete transformation of the landscape – mountains engulfed, waterfalls and rivers, including the St. Maurice, vanishing, and deep crevices opening in the land.

The insert map pinpoints the earthquake epicentres 1954-1962 in Ontario and Quebec along the St. Lawrence and Ottawa valleys. This region has experienced many hundreds of earthquakes of varying magnitude over the last three hundred years.

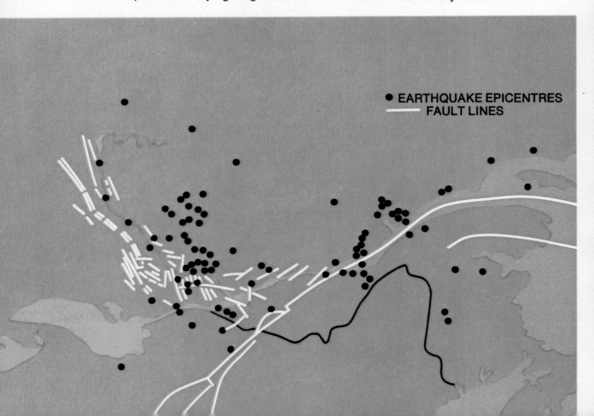

● EARTHQUAKE EPICENTRES
— FAULT LINES

◄ *Faults are cracks in otherwise solid rock caused by opposing underground pressure within the earth's crust. Some faults extend for hundreds of miles along the valley floor.*

► *Horst and graben are the technical terms for long troughs and flat-topped ridges that are bounded by parallel faults with vertical movement. The Ottawa valley contains the latter type of fault.*

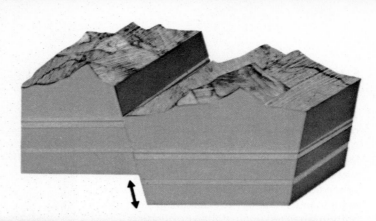

Mountains on the plain

The Monteregian Hills lie in the St. Lawrence river valley and extend from Montreal to the Appalachian uplands. Eight peaks in all – Mount Royal, St. Bruno, Beloeil, Rougemont, Yamaska, Shefford, Brome and Johnson – they would normally be considered mere mounds in mountainous country, but assume greater proportion when set against the surrounding flatness of the land. Named after the Latin *Mons Regius*, Royal Mountain, the most famed of the peaks, they look, from the air, like an irregularly curved crescent running from east to west. Mount Johnson, the eighth mountain, stands between the two points of the crescent. The hills shoot up in conical fashion to a considerable height above the surrounding lowlands (individual elevations range from St. Bruno's 715 feet to Brome's altitude of 1755 feet). The Monteregians are composed of igneous rocks thrust upwards through igneous action which intruded upon the existing sedimentary rock layers during the Cretaceous period. The presence of sea shells in old shorelines around the hills suggests that these hills were at one stage partly submerged beneath the Champlain Sea.

MONTREAL

LAKE CHAMPLAIN

◄ *Many millions of years ago, igneous rocks intruded upward into the softer and older sedimentary rock layers which had been laid down in the Saint Lawrence valley.*

► *After many millions of years of erosion, the sedimentary rocks have been largely worn away, leaving the hard igneous intrusions projecting above the plains.*

▲ An aerial shot captures the crescent formation of the Monteregian Hills spreading out from Mount Royal in the centre of Montreal.

► Some Monteregian Hills, as the one in the photo, show twin domes, which reflect variations in this composition of the rocks.

Overleaf:
Layers of clay were laid down in the Champlain Sea in the area that is now the St. Lawrence valley. Note the red lichen covering the shale.

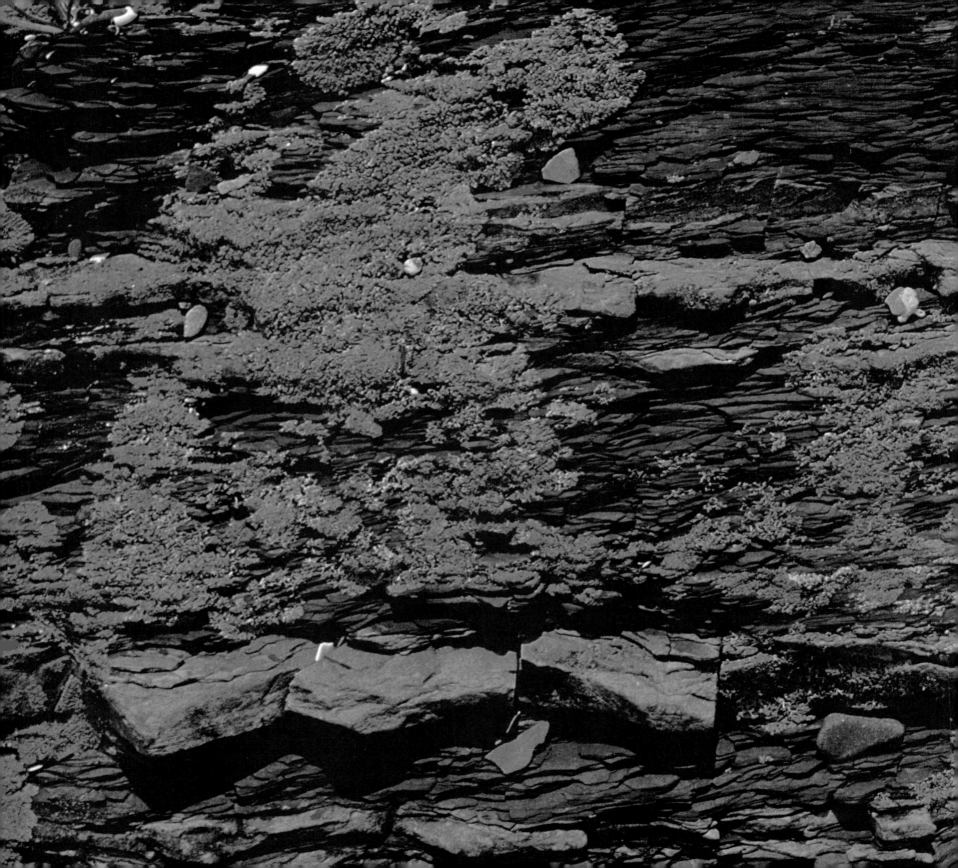

PART TWO / GEOLOGY

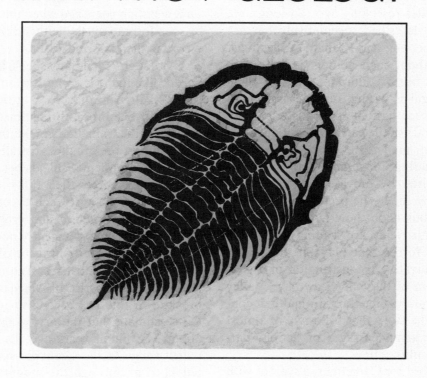

4 THE FORMATION OF THE VALLEY

Some rivers carve their own valleys, like the Colorado or the Niagara. Others, like the Rhine or the Saint Lawrence, flow through valleys made long before the rivers found them, and these have more eventful histories. The events that led to the present Saint Lawrence Valley, for instance, began with the rise of a mountain system now called the Grenville Province of the Canadian Shield. The Grenvilles rose long ago. So long ago, indeed, that their rise can be described speculatively but not factually. "At best," says the eminent Canadian geologist J. Tuzo Wilson, "our ideas about such matters as mountain building are still vague. If our basic assumption that the earth as a whole has been fairly rigid is wrong, our ideas need revision and much of what has been written about historical and structural geology . . . and physics of the earth is out of date."

These uncertainties have made an exciting time for geologists, who have been reading imaginative new meanings into data painstakingly acquired by previous generations of their colleagues; and they have made the present a promising time for anybody who is curious about how his world works, since the speculation and controversy are leading to a more flexible understanding of the forces that play on the earth's crust. For the moment, the narrative reconstruction of a geological event like the formation of the Saint Lawrence Valley may be something closer to semi-documentary drama than conventional academic history. The story that follows will almost certainly turn out to include some passages of fiction; particularly since it opens in Precambrian time.

Precambrian is a loaded word for Canadians, a symbol with the power of a totem and the density of the stone subcontinent it describes. We use it interchangeably with the word for our nationality: Precambrian Shield, Canadian Shield. Our human history has been scratched on Precambrian rock, our sense of the earth's look and feel imposed on us by Precambrian shapes and textures. Many of us close our eyes, and see a particular Precambrian landscape of bowed granitic rockfaces and dark, bent pines. All these images, feelings and meanings run together in a kind of emotional rhetoric; by contrast, the narrative of the native rock is recorded in a dry, broken code. Here Precambrian is merely the designation for a period of time longer than thought and dimmer than hindsight.

By the guess most geologists seem to favour at the moment, the earth is about five billion years old. There are signs in the rock, mainly fossils and decomposing minerals, that carry the geological record back in some detail for about six hundred million years. This is the outer frontier of a period known as the Cambrian. Precambrian describes the trackless slope of time that runs backward from the beginning of the Cambrian period —a few billion years ago when the face of the earth was wrinkled by rock formations that either disappeared or incorporated little record of their rise and decline.

Although Canadians speak habitually of *the* Precambrian Shield, like the sole owners of an exclusive property, there is a shield of Precambrian rock at the geological nucleus of every continent. The Precambrian Shield of Africa is more than twice the size of the Canadian Shield; there is almost as much exposed Precambrian rock in the Australian Shield as in our own. They are called continental shields because they tend to take slightly domed shape across their full width and breadth, but they are not simple structures. Each was fused from many parts by the successive construction and erosion of several mountain systems. Seven such systems have now been traced in the Canadian Shield, and they may have involved the rise and fall of forty separate mountain ranges. The oldest of these systems is now known as the Superior province of the Shield. By estimating the breakdown rate or radioactive minerals in the rock, geophysicists estimate that the first range of the Superior system rose about 3.2 billion years ago. By the same measure, the most recent range of the Grenville system, the last province of the Shield to go through the mountain-building cycle, apparently rose about eight hundred million years ago. This is not to say that the Superior rock is two and a half billion years older than the Grenville rock; only that the inner structure of the rock was changed—recrystallized—at times roughly that far apart.

By the time the Grenville system matured, the mountains of the older provinces were no doubt largely dismantled by erosion. The Grenville ranges probably dominated the southeastern margin of the continental nucleus much as the ranges of the Cordillera dominate the western margin of the continent now.

The peaks of the Grenvilles were probably at that time between ten and twenty thousand feet high; the Grenville system was a thousand miles long and about two hundred miles wide. Its shape has reminded many geological writers of a canoe.

Below the bow, the outline of the canoe is marred by a bulbous protrusion at the end of a thinner neck. The neck is known to geologists as the Frontenac Axis, and the much larger bulb is known as the Adirondack Dome. Both seem to have gone through the mountain-building cycle at about the same time as the nearby Grenville ranges. They may be an integral part of an original "Grenville formation," later separated from the main structure by the collapse of an intervening wedge of rock, although from their height and shape some geologists have concluded that they were built in a separate pulse of the earth's crust. In either case, traces in the rock tell something of what happened in the heat and pressure of the event itself.

The dominant rock of the Frontenac Axis is a coarse-grained variety of marble—sedimentary rock that was originally formed at the bottom of a Precambrian sea as limestone, and then crystallized by the upheaval in the earth's crust that raised the Axis. But near the present Canadian bank of the river, in a belt about six miles wide and twenty long, the marble becomes relatively scarce. Here the dominant rock is a pink medium-grained variety of granite, known as Rockport granite. Interlaced with the Rockport granite at several places is a second pinkish granitic rock, so coarse-grained that it has the texture of mortar; this variety is called Frontenac granite.

Near Rockfield, Ontario, there is a large, coarse-grained pavement of Frontenac granite with rounded dapples of finer grained rock contained within it. The dapples are intrusions of Rockport granite. Half a mile away there is a second granite pavement, this one a fine-grained pavement containing coarse-grained dapples. The roles are reversed; the pavement is Rockport granite, the intrusions are Frontenac granite. The two kinds of granite switch roles like this at several nearby places. Here and there they even seem to merge into a hybrid rock combining both types.

From these observations the geologist who made them, H. R. Wynne-Edwards of Queen's University, believes he may be able to reconstruct one detail of the process that erected the Frontenac Axis. The two granites could only have alternated roles the way they did, he reasons, if they were both flowing at the same general stage. At any precise moment or place, though, one would have been more mobile than the other. This, he says, is an unusual way for two granites that vary sharply in chemical and mineral structure to come into contact with each other. How did it happen? Perhaps, Wynne-Edwards says, like this: the minerals of the Frontenac granite seem to have formed originally with very little water around, probably deep in the rock basement of the region. The Rockport granite shows signs of having incorporated far more water, and may have originated as part of a sandstone layer deposited somewhere above the basement on the floor of the sea. During the convulsive upthrust of the mountain-building cycle, the deeply bedded basement rock migrated upward. Meanwhile, the heat and pressure of the convulsion crystallized the overlying bed of sandstone, changing it in turn to granite. Finally, far above the levels where each began, the two mobile varieties of granite encountered each other and interlaced, here the Rockport granite intruding on the Frontenac, there the reverse.

By this account, the Frontenac granite was already part of an old, buried, apparently stable body of rock when the Rockport stone was deposited far above it. But dated by the decay of their radioactive minerals, both granites are the same age—something just under a billion years—since they were last recrystallized at the same time. Whether or not this theory turns out to be sound, it demonstrates on a scale small enough to be seen and touched, the large uncertainties involved in speaking of Precambrian rock.

However the Grenville rocks may have formed their combinations, they eventually incorporated the marble and granites described here, along with almost every variety of rock known, from brown lava to greenstone, from dun sandstone to sparkling quartzite. The mountains they formed yielded in time to the appetites of erosion, so that half a billion years ago the long southwest strike of the Grenvilles where they met the sea had been levelled to a stone plateau, perhaps not much higher than the present hills. To the south the Frontenac Axis and the Adirondack dome, similarly worn, curved back towards the east to form a stone embayment. On the floor of the bay and along the submarine shelf that sloped from the Grenville coast, the sea began to deposit the silts that built new layers of stone.

The Precambrian Shield includes all the surface exposures of Precambrian rock that outcrop in a gigantic horseshoe around Hudson Bay. But subsurface rock formed during the Precambrian eon slopes away from the rim of the Shield in all directions. This is the basement structure of the present continent and the undersea shelves that reach out from either coast. Much of this buried Precambrian rock is sedimentary, deposited layer by layer on the ocean floor by currents bearing silt washed down from the eroding mountains of the Shield—a case of Precambrian rock engendering more Precambrian rock.

Among the causes of the collapse and upheaval that create new mountain ranges is the accumulation of a greater weight of rock than the crust below can bear. New sedimentary rock, much of it built from debris eroded from the Grenvilles and the older provinces of the Shield, contributed to the rise of the next great North American mountain system, the Appalachians. And with the upthrust of the first major Appalachian range, the third stone wall of what is now the Saint Lawrence Valley was locked in place.

The earliest pulse of mountain-building energy probably ran through the crust of the Appalachian region before the end of the Precambrian eon; the latest, about 250 million years afterward. Unlike the anonymous ranges of the Grenville system, the successive Appalachian ranges have been named and described separately. East of the Adirondack dome and south of the main Grenville coastline rose the Taconic Mountains. In their prime the peaks of the Taconics were probably the equals of the modern Rockies, butted at the northern end of the range against the outlying shelves of the Grenville system, and reaching two thousand miles to the southwest. Then erosion cut them down. In the end, erosion is a stronger natural force than the cataclysmic energy that builds mountains. Freeze and thaw, the rub of wind, water and ice, the decay of mineral compounds attacked by oxygen—grain by grain the rock rots.

Debris from the eroding Taconics washed down the mountain flanks and accumulated on the floors of the surrounding seas, forming new layers of sedimentary rock. Now and then a fresh pulse of mountain-building energy ran through the region, and the cycle began again. At times the main source of the new mountain rock was apparently lava from volcano clusters off the east coast, at others it was sandstone or limestone heaved

from the ocean floor; at others it was a granite seemingly intruded by plastic flow from a deep zone in the earth's crust called plutonic granite, after the mythic dukedom of the deep regions.

Such spasm brought the northern frontier of the Taconic range up against the southern margin of the Grenville system. Some geologists speak of the encounter as a "clash" between contending forces of rock, the mobile young Taconics thrusting upward with great force, the stable, deeply rooted mass of the Grenvilles absorbing the shock without yielding. This vivid scenario may be overdrawn; the lines of cleavage between the Taconic and Grenville formations have been interpreted in several ways, none conclusive.

Between the old and the new mountain systems the sea entered, even before the last tremors of the mountain-building period had made their final folds in the Taconic rock. Penetrating the corridor separating the two rock systems, the salt water reached a thousand miles southwest to the higher ground of the Frontenac Axis. At the base of the corridor the sea began again, in its repetitive way, to lay down fresh layers of rock-forming sediments from the eroding mountains on either side. From time to time the level of the ocean fell in relation to the crust of the continent, and the sea withdrew. At these times the long corridor into the continental interior probably began to look, in outline at least, like an ancestral version of the Saint Lawrence Valley. Rain or melting snow, the runoff from the Grenville plateau and the flank of the Taconic Mountains, probably followed the corridor to the Atlantic in ancestral rivers heavy with red-brown mud. Then the sea rose, and paved the valley floor with another layer of sediments that eventually became new rock.

The new rock obliterated any trace of these ancestral rivers, if indeed such rivers ever ran, but the rock carries traces of other kinds. From fossils embedded in the rock, its mineral structure and chemical behaviour, the Geological Survey of Canada has concluded that the sea advanced to the head of the valley, withdrew and advanced again, at least eight times. During these invasions the sea deposited sediments that later formed sixteen distinguishable varieties of rock in the central basin of the valley. By a kind of geological accident, fragments of all sixteen varieties are grouped in a natural outdoor display on St. Helen's Island, in the Saint Lawrence River off Montreal. The display, a

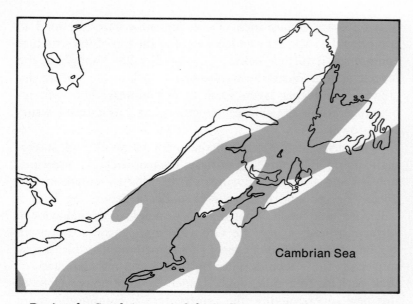
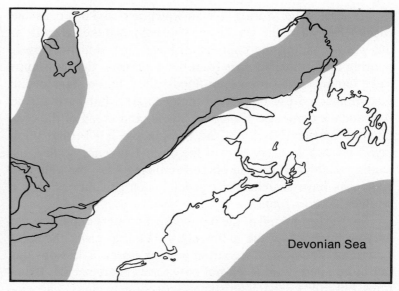

During the Cambrian period the St. Lawrence valley was partially covered by prehistoric seas (shown above). By the Devonian period the sea covered almost the entire valley. The sediments laid down by these seas formed much of the geological structure of the valley today.

museum with neither walls nor curators, is a mosaic of broken rock shards bedded in a very hard natural cement. This mixture, called breccia, ran north and south across the island in a strip the colour of burnt orange peel, a mile long and almost half a mile wide, until the island was remade to accommodate Expo 67. Here and there, the mixture contains chunks of sandstone, limestone, shale and dolomite belonging to each of the sixteen varieties of sedimentary rock that have been identified in this section of the valley. Finally, at the north end of the mosaic near the river, there are two huge blocks of fossil-bearing limestone less than four hundred million years old. (Both are now concealed by Expo construction.) These are the youngest rocks in the breccia and, indeed, the youngest that have been discovered anywhere in the valley. Not that these limestone boulders necessarily belong to the final layer of sedimentary stone deposited on the valley floor by the invading sea. But if there were more recent layers, as most geologists assume there must have been, all trace of them has been stripped away by erosion.

Nor do the beds of sedimentary rock that remain in place cover the valley floor in uniform layers. Toward the head of the valley, near the Frontenac Axis, the Geological Survey has measured deposits of sedimentary rock two thousand feet thick

at their deepest point—compared to ten thousand feet in the Montreal section of the valley.

Shallower seas, it seems, reached the head of the valley for shorter periods of time. There were two reasons for this, one of them very simple. From the Frontenac Axis the valley floor sloped toward the low central basin. The drop is still over two hundred feet in about a hundred miles, and may well have been more a few hundred million years ago. When the ocean level rose, the advancing sea naturally mounted this slope slowly, after it had flooded the central basin; when the ocean level fell, the sea retreated first from the higher ground near the Axis. Several times the level of the ocean rose so high that salt water submerged the Frontenac Axis altogether. The sea at these stages deposited rock-building sediments all the way from the Saint Lawrence Valley to the continental interior. But even during these great floods the sea was shallower over the relatively high ground of the Frontenac Axis, and withdrew earlier. The first of these continental seas, for example, left behind a rock layer sixteen hundred feet thick in the Montreal section of the valley. Toward the head of the valley at the Axis, the same layer, called the Beekmantown, was only a little more than three hundred feet thick.

At least once, during a high-water period known as the Black River stage, the sea seems to have flooded the valley from the west—invading the continental basin first, and then overpouring the Frontenac Axis from the depression that now cups Lake Ontario. And even later floods, the Clinton stage of the sea, submerged not only the Frontenac Axis but parts of the Adirondack dome, the Canadian Shield, and much of the continental interior. No doubt the Clinton sea left behind thick layers of rock in every part of the Saint Lawrence Valley, including the highest ground of the Frontenac Axis; but although geologists have searched energetically for generations, not a boulder has been found.

So the rise and fall of the ocean level accounts in part for the varying thickness of the sedimentary rock that paves the Saint Lawrence Valley. The second important reason is less obvious but more interesting. Rock not only forms characteristic structures, but follows characteristic patterns of behaviour. The geological history of the Saint Lawrence Valley starts with the way the rock took shape, but includes the way the rock behaved—and is behaving still.

On their own time scale, the immoveable peaks of the immemorial mountains act something like an ice-cube melting in a water-glass. The continental bedrock is perhaps twenty-five miles deep. The substructure of the ocean floor is much thinner, possibly less than five miles deep, and made of heavier rock, probably basalt. Together, the continental and ocean substructures make up the earth's "crust"—a confusing choice of words, since the crust rides on a zone of denser, more rigid rock. This underlying rock zone, known as the earth's mantle, is about eighteen hundred miles deep and accounts for something like eighty-five percent of the globe's volume. The mantle in turn encloses an outer core of molten iron around an inner core of solid iron.

Shock waves moving through these buried structures traverse roughly two miles of sandstone in a second, four miles of granite, almost five miles of mantle rock. From these and other observations, many geologists now suspect the mantle rock to be dunite, a complex silicate material heavy with iron and magnesium. Deep in the substructure, the weight of the overlying rock builds up great pressures; at twenty-five miles, the border between the continental crust and the mantle is squeezed by eighty tons on every square inch. These pressures naturally tend to compress the rock. Any added weight at the top of the structure compresses it further below. Less predictable, though, is the reverse action. When the weight of the rock at the surface decreases, the deeper layers seem to decompress. The rock rebounds, raising the surface structures even as erosion wears them down.

Geophysicists describe this behavior by an elegant mathematical principle known as isostasy: the tendency of downward, upward and sideways pressures on the rock to remain in balance. The rebound of deep rock under a decreasing load is called isostatic recoil. Applying this principle to the behavior of surface structures like the Grenville and Taconic mountain systems, the sequence of events goes something like this: a new range, say the Taconics, piles up folded and refolded slabs of rock perhaps four miles high. Under the enormous weight of this new superstructure, the substructure is compressed more densely than it was before the mountain-building convulsions began. Simultaneously the forces of erosion attack the newly exposed mountain rock. Water and ice carry away decomposing minerals, which elsewhere become new layers of sedimentary rock. Within about fifty million years, the mountains are reduced to a stone plateau. But during the same fifty million years the compressed rock of the substructure, released gradually from the weight of the mature range, has been recoiling toward the surface.

The Taconics were continually renewed throughout their destruction, until at the end they were completely levelled and the pressures on the subsurface rock were once more in their original state of balance, or isostasy.

Like the Taconics, the later Appalachian ranges that locked the current blocks of stone into the southerly wall of the Saint Lawrence Valley warped the valley floor in alternating directions. In maturity the mountains bore down the floor by their great weight, making the valley a natural corridor for the sea; in their eroding old age they released the rock below to rebound upward. During the long intervals of upthrust, the rising floor tipped the sea gradually back toward the Atlantic basin. Withdrawing first from the higher ground of the Frontenac Axis region, the sea left behind shallower layers of sedimentary rock in the upper valley, deeper layers in the central valley.

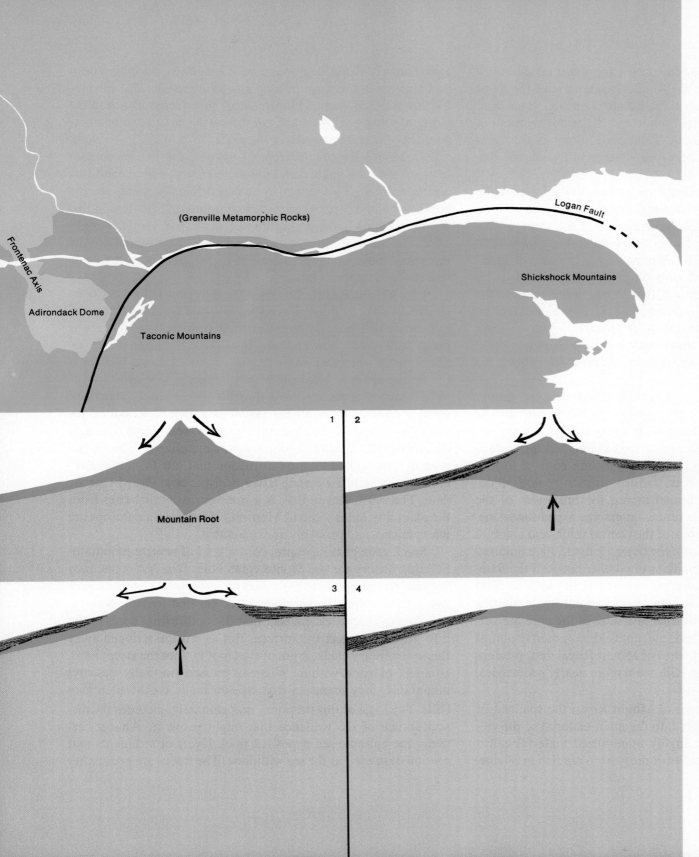

Frontenac Axis

(Grenville Metamorphic Rocks)

Logan Fault

Adirondack Dome

Shickshock Mountains

Taconic Mountains

1 | 2

Mountain Root

3 | 4

Over most of its course east of the Frontenac Axis the St. Lawrence river flows along the Logan Fault. This large break in the earth's crust marks the contact between the Grenville metamorphic rocks of the Canadian shield and the Palaeozoic formations. Some of these rocks were deformed by the Taconic Revolution, while others were deformed later in time. The Logan Fault, sometimes called the Logan Line, dates from these events and has been etched out to form a valley by erosion. The St. Lawrence river developed its present course in the valley upon the withdrawal of the last of the glaciers.

ISOSTASY

When compressive forces within the earth produce mountains, these same huge forces also squeeze a part of the earth's crust and thicken it so that the mountains have roots. As erosion tears away the peaks, the root rises. This is the process of isostasy. The diagram (1) shows a mountain undergoing erosion, in (2) eroded sediments have accumulated away from the mountain and, because the weight has decreased, the root has risen. In (3) the process has continued until (4) no root is present.

53

The most recent pulse of the convulsive energy that raises mountains probably ran through the southerly ramparts of the Saint Lawrence Valley more than three hundred million years ago. Between the end of that final tremor and the relatively modern episode of the great ice age, the geological history of the Saint Lawrence Valley is unrecorded—a reverberating silence disturbed by a local mystery.

The mystery broke the silence somewhere toward the middle of that long blank corridor of time. About a hundred million years ago an arc of minor igneous intrusions, none seem to have been a true volcano, blistered the valley floor. They have been named the Monteregian Hills—Mount Royal, the core of Montreal, and seven others: Mounts Saint Bruno, Saint Hillaire, Rougemont, Yamaska, Shefford, Brome and, a few miles to the south of the arc, Johnson (or Mount Saint Gregoire, as it is often called in the contemporary mood of Quebec). The hills are roughly circular or oval in shape, and in their present condition rise between six hundred and fifteen hundred feet above the valley floor.

From the visible rock of a typical member of the group, such as Mount Royal, the inner cores of the hills would appear to be shafts of very dense subsurface stone, driven straight upward in a plastic state under pressures that humped the surface layers of sedimentary rock. In the interesting case of Mount Royal this assumption has been verified, as such geological deductions rarely are, by a tunnel driven the full width of the mountain near its base. The tunnel enters upwarped limestone, passes into the dense hard rock of the central shaft, and emerges through a layer of limestone on the opposite flank. Five hundred feet above, on both sides, the lines of contact between the limestone and the hard inner core are exposed at the surface; they are almost exactly above the lines of contact cut by the tunnel. For this five hundred feet, at least, the sides of the core are vertical. Among the distorted folds and antifolds common to almost all upthrust rocks, the erect cores of Mount Royal and, presumably, the other Monteregian Hills seem more nearly geometrical than geological.

In the northeast quadrant of Mount Royal the roadbed of Houde Boulevard cuts deeply into the main material of the volcanic core, a dark, heavy, highly mineralized material called gabbro. Here and there, patches of the gabbro are rich in olivine,

a particularly dense compound of silica, iron and magnesium that appears in the form of long greenish crystals. The olivine-bearing material, named Montrealite, bears a resemblance to the material some geologists believe the earth's mantle to be composed of—the basic material of the globe.

At Mount Royal's Northern Lookout, the line of contact between the dark gabbro and the sedimentary rock around it is clearly marked. This second rock was originally shale, but the hot thrust of the core baked it to the hardness of flint, and in this form it is called hornfels. Eighty feet north, the hornfels breaks off at the line of contact with a third rock. This was originally limestone, now changed to marble in the same way the shale was changed to hornfels.

Like Mount Royal, the other Monteregian Hills have been analyzed for their mineral content, mapped for their structural intricacies and puzzled over for their origins. The mystery is pretty well intact; how and why they came to blister the valley floor exactly when and where they did are not known. Neither is the origin of three local outcrops of breccia that are thought to be somehow associated with the hills. These are collections of stone fragments from all the layers of valley rock, bound together by a kind of hard natural cement. One of them, on Saint Helen's Island, was described in the previous chapter. The second is an outcrop called Pointe-du-Buisson that juts from the south bank of the Saint Lawrence River near the new Hydro-Quebec dam. The third, Covey Hill, is a stone curiosity that rises from the plain fifty miles south of Montreal. The breccia outcrops are unexplained, and probably unexplainable.

Some geologists have proposed a kind of reverse mountain-building history for the Monteregian Hills. The hot cores, they suggest, thrust upward into a bed of sedimentary rock at least two thousand feet thicker than the layers that remain. So deep was the covering rock, indeed, that the upthrusting cores of the hills never did break the surface. But as erosion stripped away this sedimentary cloak, it uncovered foot by foot the steep, hard, columns of rock within. Whereas erosion normally destroys mountains, they maintain that erosion made the Monteregian Hills. The logic of this proposal, unfortunately, includes the disappearance of the evidence that might prove it. Almost certainly the episodic sea deposited thick layers of sediments that erosion destroyed as the sea withdrew. The traces are gone; after

RIVER OF ICE

In winter the entire length of the St. Lawrence River is subjected to freezing temperatures. Kingston, Ontario, at the south-western end of the river, is 150 miles further south than Quebec City at the north-eastern end. Ice conditions become steadily more intense as the river flows northward and the ports of Montreal and Quebec are among the first to be closed to navigation by ice in early January.

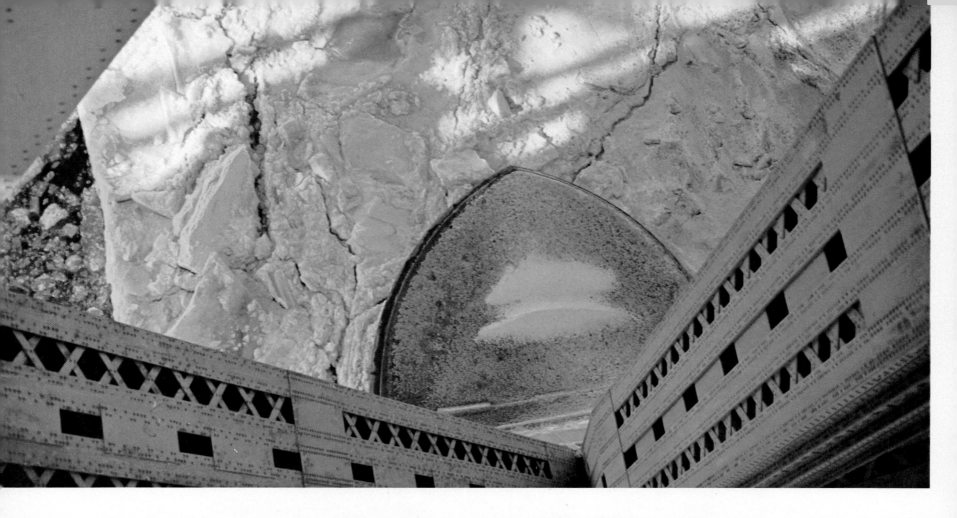

Spring break up

The port of Quebec, at the mouth of the Gulf of St. Lawrence, experiences average winter temperatures eight to ten degrees lower than more southerly Toronto. The resulting ice formation in the river is added to by the continued progression of ice floating down the river toward the sea. Modern ice-breakers have added considerably to the port's open season but the ice still closes it for several months each year and does considerable damage to the docks and off-shore port facilities.

▲ *Bridge supports are particularly susceptible to the immense pressures which the river ice is capable of exerting. This support, at Quebec City, is shaped in the form of a triangle to split the ice sheet and cause it to flow around the base of the bridge.*

◄ *Modern icebreakers, like the Montcalm, are able to penetrate the heaviest ice flows and prevent them from doing major damage. The icebreaker slides forward over the surface of the heavy ice and the weight of the ship breaks through to the water below.*

56

The plant life and soil formation along these shores are subjected to intense scouring from the moving, flowing ice.

► The spring break-up of river ice occurs in March or April. The river fills with melting ice floating toward the sea.

Overleaf:
Spring floods like this are a frequent re-sult of the rapid melting of the winter ice.

Smaller streams are as affected by the ice as is the Saint Lawrence. Here the ice cover remains coated on the trees.

the curious advent of the Monteregian Hills the geological record reverted to silence for about another hundred million years.

The silence was finally broken by the quietest event imaginable, a slow, invisible change in the environment. The average annual temperature of the earth began to fall, at first almost imperceptibly. Plant fossils suggest that for half a billion years the mean temperature may have been almost constant, slightly above seventy degrees. Toward the end of an epoch called the Paleocene, perhaps fifty million years ago, a cooling trend set in, and when the mean temperature of the globe had fallen to about fifty degrees, the ice advanced. The date is obscure; perhaps a million years ago, or perhaps half that. The causes are speculative. But the results are vivid and contemporary, since the glaciers and the waterbodies that attended them became the landscapers of the Saint Lawrence Valley.

More precisely, the fourth stage of the ice age landscaped the valley. Traces of three earlier advances and withdrawals can be discerned in the Saint Lawrence region, but only faintly. Each reworked the ground, so that the valley profile described here is essentially the work of the most recent glacial stage, which has been named the Wisconsin. Nor did the Wisconsin glacial stage develop in a single episode of advance and withdrawal; there is evidence of several substages during which lobes of ice invaded the south, retreated toward one side or the other of Hudson Bay, and invaded again, usually readvancing in a somewhat different direction.

The first such advance of the Wisconsin stage began about one hundred thousand years ago. For the opening sixty thousand years of this stage, as during the previous stages of the ice age, the glaciers in withdrawal released deluges of fresh water along their melting southern flanks. Accumulating in great natural basins toward the center of the continent, these glacial floods created a succession of freshwater seas, ancestral Great Lakes whose features were largely eradicated by later glaciers. Unimaginable torrents of water spilled from the glacial lakes across the continent to the oceans, wherever they found the easiest

Geological maps of the Monteregian Hills depicted on P. 44-45 show: 1. Alnoite 2. Ijolite 3. Okaite 4. Carbonatite 5. Nepheline Syenite 6. Pulaskite 7. Nordmarkite 8. Syenite Porphyry-Breccia 9. Hybrid Rocks 10. Essexite 11. Gabbro 12. Peridotite.

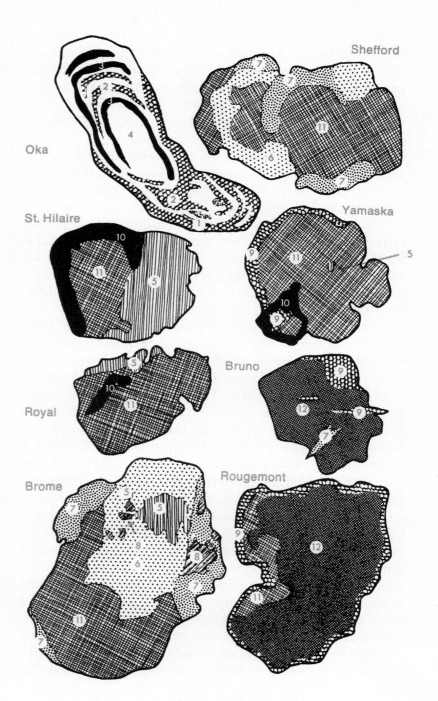

route—west and south through the early Mississippi system, east and south through the Mohawk and Hudson valleys. But unless the traces have been completely erased, or generations of geologists have entirely overlooked them, at no time did the swollen interglacial lakes of the continental interior find a passage to the sea through the Saint Lawrence Valley. Presumably the Frontenac Axis plugged the entrance, and the valley seems to have remained a natural watercourse without a river, until a long withdrawal of the Wisconsin glacial stage, about forty thousand years ago, known as the Saint Pierre interval.

At the time, the climate in the valley seems to have warmed until it was only slightly cooler than it is now, an intriguingly precise calculation made by studying the wood in peat beds near Three Rivers. The ice is thought to have retreated far north on the Canadian Shield, and the runoff from the melting glaciers appears to have followed the Ottawa Valley to the Saint Lawrence, and the Saint Lawrence Valley to the sea. There developed at this time, says the Geological Survey of Canada, "a drainage system comparable to that of the present Saint Lawrence system."

If these rivers were indeed the first to make the Saint Lawrence Valley their channel to the sea, their earliest appearance was a relatively short one. Within a few thousand years the ice sheet advanced again. The residual evidence indicates that the westerly lobe overwhelmed the Frontenac Axis, wheeled against the flank of the Adirondack Dome and raked the valley from southwest to northeast. In the Axis the ice scored and polished the rough outcrops of granite, and stripped away any loose cover that might have accumulated in previous ages. So that, in the river yet to come, bare knobs of granite called The Thousand Islands would break the surface of the water, and in the fields on the north shore a thousand similar "island" knobs would break the surface of clay beds not deposited until after the ice made its last retreat. The eastern lobe of the ice cap moved south from Labrador and northern Quebec on a broad front, filled the valley, thrust against the Appalachian Wall to the south, and diverged in two streams, one northeast to invade the ocean shelf, the other southwest to penetrate the valley. Meanwhile local ice-fields formed at the high points of the Adirondack and Appalachian uplands, glacial tongues put out to the north and merged with the main lobes. Eventually the ice overrode the valley altogether, along with the highlands to the south; from the air only a mottled, cracked plain of ice would have been visible, with the highest rock perhaps two miles below its surface. This seems to have been the outlook over the Saint Lawrence Valley eighteen thousand years ago, at the peak of the Wisconsin glacial stage. Since then, with minor fluctuations, the ice has been retreating.

Ice carves and covers the land in a variety of peculiar shapes, with names that are a familiar, vivid, but often hazy part of the Canadian vocabulary: words like esker and drumlin, kame and moraine. All of them are glacial deposits composed of till—a catch-all name for an unsorted mixture of silts, clays, sands, gravels, stones and boulders released from the ice in an almost endless variety of proportions and colours. Advancing, the glacier scoured the surface of fine stone particles broken down by weathering, and of loose rocks and boulders. The boulders became cutting edges on the underside of the glacier, gouging the surface rock more or less deeply depending on how hard it was. These scrapings the glacier incorporated, too; and within the ice mass forward movement tended to grind the stone fragments one against the other. Finally, in retreat, the glacier released a paste of pulverised rock, an amalgam lumpy with larger particles that ranged in size from grains of sand to boulders twenty feet and more across, which we call till.

Glacial till encrusts all of Montreal Island except a fringe of one riverbank and the top of Mount Royal. Even here a small beach of Beaver Lake, on the mountain's concave summit, is paved with till under a thin layer of sand—evidence that when the glaciers finally withdrew, they probably left the valley varnished with a patchwork coat of till from end to end and top to bottom. In retreat, though, the ice was no more constant than in advance, so that fluctuations of the ice edge left three separate varieties of till on Montreal Island, and an uncounted, probably uncountable, number throughout the valley.

Water working on the glacial till, sorting the fragments by size and weight and sifting them, here and there, into consistent beds, formed the soil of the valley. At first, during the final retreat of the ice, the water was fresh, the runoff of the melting glaciers. Clay soil laid down by fresh water in this climate usually carries a striking code of identification, a laminated pattern of horizontal layers with the coarsest grains at the bottom of each layer, the finest at the top. The laminations are annual, like the rings of a tree. They are accounted for in this case by the freezing temperatures of winter, which slowed or stopped the movement of silt until the following spring. Clays so marked are said to be varved. Small beds of varved clay scatter the valley from the Frontenac Axis to Quebec City, beds so small they are evidence mainly of the relative unimportance of fresh water in forming the present soil of the valley.

Most of the valley clay was sifted and spread by salt water advancing from the Atlantic as the ice withdrew. The ocean level was rising, fed by glacial spilloff throughout the northern hemisphere. Moreover, the continental crust of the northeast quadrant had been greatly depressed by the weight of the ice sheet; the floor of the Saint Lawrence Valley was at least seven hundred feet lower than it is now. But the valley floor began to rise as the ice load decreased. Much as the mountain roots described in the previous chapter were thrust upward by isostatic recoil during periods of erosion, isostatic recoil now lifted the regions that had been borne down by the ice cap. In this case the recoil lifted the land surfaces with incommensurable speed; a cycle that had taken millions of years in response to eroding rock now took thousands of years in response to melting ice.

Cupped in such an erratic basin, the sea that pressed into the lowlands behind the retreating ice barely had time to establish one shore line before the basin tilted, sloshing the surface of the sea against a new beach. The lowest marine beaches carved on the slopes of the valley by the post-glacial sea are now not much more than one hundred feet above sea level; the highest, a little over seven hundred feet. The oldest were cut and covered with sand or gravel very close to 11,300 years ago, the youngest about fifteen hundred years later. This post-glacial sea, really a large, spiked bay of the ocean, has been named the Champlain Sea.

The short, unstable history of the Champlain Sea accounts for a maze of terraces and beaches, a profusion of sand banks, clay beds and gravel drifts in every reach of the valley. So widely, indeed, did the sea rework the landscape that the geological time scale seems at first to be thrown out of joint—fifteen hundred years for this sculptural transformation, and tens of millions for changes less conspicuous? Well, yes; but by a slight shift of chronological perspective, the contradiction can be seen to connect firmly enough with earlier events, and may even help to make the entire geological narrative more coherent. This shift is a matter of enlarging the present—this moment, geologically speaking—to include the Champlain Sea. Within this perspective, the gravel, sand and clay deposits of the Champlain Sea are the contemporary beginnings of future generations of sedimentary rocks. Like similar beds left behind by episodic seas again and again since the unlit opening of Precambrian time, the rich clay fields and wooded till ridges sifted by the currents of the Champlain Sea will become in their turn limestone, or sandstone, or perhaps the fine paste of a new glacial till.

PATTERN OF SETTLEMENT

The air photograph at right clearly shows the long strip farms which were established by the early settlers along the St. Lawrence river. Each farm was thus provided with access to the river—the major highway of the period. The fertile soils which make farming possible were laid down by the Champlain Sea. Note the highway running along the shore of the St. Lawrence.

5 THE FORMATION OF THE RIVER

"The present Saint Lawrence River," according to Professor J. A. Elson of the McGill University geology department, "established its course about eight thousand years ago." Professor Elson seems to be alone in having made a direct estimate of the river's age. He bases his calculations on the intimate structure, the "profile," of tree pollen preserved here and there in the valley, and describes his result not as an established fact but as an "inference."

Elsewhere, estimates of the river's age can only be deducted from indirect evidence and oblique references. The standard guidebook of the Geological Survey of Canada says, "As the (Champlain) sea withdrew, fluvial drainage of the present Saint Lawrence system was established." This is the guidebook's only direct reference to the age of the present river. But later, in a passage on the development of the modern Great Lakes system, the authors explain when and why the Champlain Sea withdrew. The unstable floor of the Saint Lawrence Valley, released from the weight of the ice-cap and rebounding upward, forced the Champlain Sea back to the Atlantic; at just this time, the up-lifting crust to the west brought about a late stage of the glacial Great Lakes known as the Nipissing stage.

"Radiocarbon datings of wood from Nipissing Great Lakes beaches," the guidebook says, "indicate an age of about 3,500 years." By contrast, datings of material left by the Champlain Sea itself suggest that the sea withdrew about 9,800 years ago. During the Nipissing stage, according to the guidebook, the waters of the Upper Lakes discharged mainly through outlets in the Duluth and Chicago regions, into the watershed of the Mississippi River. Some overflow from the Georgian Bay area ran down the Ottawa Valley to the central Saint Lawrence; the upper Saint Lawrence apparently drained Lakes Erie and Ontario. Finally, says the guidebook, the lakes fell to their present levels. They began to drain eastward link by link, discharging their full runoff through a single great spillway to the Atlantic, the present Saint Lawrence River. The time is uncertain, but it was "in the not too distant past."

Like the Geological Survey's guidebook, most other authori-

ties associate the rise of the river with the fall of the Champlain Sea. There are traces of a large body of fresh water, named the Lampsilis Lake, that seems to have flooded much of the Saint Lawrence Valley after the Champlain Sea withdrew. A geological consensus would probably agree that several abandoned river channels near the present juncture of the Ottawa and Saint Lawrence are less than nine thousand years old, and that the upper Saint Lawrence became the channel for the full runoff of the Great Lakes system less than three thousand years ago.

Not that the precise age of the river is a crucial question; there are even simpler questions that excite the curiosity of geologists more. The more interesting of these, perhaps, deal with the depth and shape of the channel that the river follows along the valley floor. Whether the river is nine thousand years old or less than three, it is too young in either case to have worn a deep trough through the underlying stone. Indeed, from the Frontenac Axis to Montreal the Saint Lawrence can hardly be said to flow within a channel at all. Rather, the water runs among and over countless gnarls of rock, seeking the lowest course. Where the terrain pitches steeply, so does the riverbed. These downhill stretches of the river were, of course, the cele-brated Saint Lawrence rapids. An older river would have worn a graded channel through the bedstone—making much early Canadian history less romantic and much of the Saint Lawrence Seaway unnecessary.

Near Montreal the descending river reaches sea level. The water flows more smoothly but the bed of the river is still erratic in profile and fairly shallow. At Quebec the rock scarps that have walled the valley at a distance converge to pinch the river. This is the end of the Saint Lawrence Valley. It is also, in geo-logical usage, the beginning of a second, hidden valley: the Saint Lawrence Submarine Valley, a sinuous concavity that scores the subsurface from here to the rim of the continental shelf a thousand miles away.

The submarine valley makes a modest start downstream from the Isle d'Orleans. The river widens, the riverbed slopes from either side toward a more clearly defined channel, and the depth of the water gradually increases, although nowhere to more than a few hundred feet. Then, near the mouth of the Saguenay River, the banks of the Saint Lawrence diverge sharply. The river bottom shelves off to a far greater depth. In

At Quebec City the rock scarps that form the valley wall converge to reduce the width of the river and mark the end of the St. Lawrence valley.

profile, both margins of the river slope toward a central trough, with steep walls and a fairly regular, flat base. Depths in the trough quickly reach a thousand feet. The walls of the trough diverge until, in the estuary, the trough is more than fifty miles wide. Along the trough's undulating floor, several sections are more than fifteen hundred feet below the surface of the water. These dimensions remain more or less constant as the submarine valley curves south of Anticosti Island and underpasses the Cabot Strait to reach the rim of the continental shelf.

The Saint Lawrence Submarine Valley is clearly a more prominent feature of the landscape, though an unseen one, than the familiar valley on the surface. Just as clearly, the geological narrative that accounts for the surface valley leaves the story of the great submarine trough untold. During the 1960's there had been a good deal of fresh speculation about how and why the submarine valley was formed along a thousand miles of river bottom and sea floor. This speculation usually begins with the hundred year old field notes of William Logan.

Logan was the first director of the Geological Survey of Canada. Like some of the rocks he collected, he was an uncommon specimen. He belonged to that generation of nineteenth-century scientists who were able to believe that reason was capable of penetrating the ultimate obscurities of nature; while Logan was camping in the Appalachian uplands, Darwin was at sea in the Beagle and Pasteur was at work in Paris. In Logan's case, this heroic mood infected him with a passion for work that seems incredible in a softer century.

"I was up every morning at four and five o'clock to rouse my Indians," he wrote a colleague during his survey of the Ottawa Valley. "We seldom left our work until we could no longer see distinctly, and it was often one, two and three hours after midnight before my protraction was finished and I could creep into my blanket." He looked like a man who worked these hours, too, "what with hair matted with spruce gum, a beard three months old, red, with two patches of white on one side, a pair of cracked spectacles, a red flannel shirt, a waistcoat with patches on the left pocket, where some sulphuric acid, which I carry in a small vial to try for the presence of lime in the rocks had leaked through—a jacket of moleskin, shining with grease, and trousers patched on one leg in four places and with a burned hole in the other leg; with beef boots—Canada boots as they are called—torn and roughened all over with scraping on the stumps and branches of trees, and patched on the legs with sundry pieces of leather of diverse colours, (and) a broad brimmed and round topped hat, once white but now no colour and battered into all shapes."

So dressed, short, hairy and hyperactive, Logan spent a great deal of time during the late 1840's chipping at large slabs of rock with a small hammer in the valley south of Montreal. Altogether he made an uncommon spectacle, and he was fond of telling his friends about times when rural onlookers had taken him for a lunatic. The result of these seemingly demented rituals he later published in a particularly coherent account of a

long fracture zone where the rock was mangled, twisted and broken, a classic example of the structure known as a rock "fault." The classic fault described by Logan comes to the surface in Pennsylvania, then runs north through the Hudson Valley and the basin of Lake Champlain to the Saint Lawrence Valley south of Montreal, where it bends east toward Quebec City; near Quebec the fault dips below the surface of the Saint Lawrence, and strikes along the riverbed toward the sea.

The sheared and mangled rocks along this fault, Logan concluded, mark a zone where mobile rock of the Appalachian system, rising in new mountain ranges, met outlying beds of the older, more stable rock structures to the west and north. In his most important book, *The Geology of Canada*, Logan, who was by now Sir William, called the fault zone he had discovered the "Appalachian Front." Later generations of geologists have tended to call it Logan's Fault, and their attempts to account for the Saint Lawrence Submarine Valley usually begin by citing

William Logan, one of the most famous Canadian geologists, was a pioneer in the geological exploration of the St. Lawrence valley.

Logan's line is a group of faults where softer rocks are mangled. The structure is a key to understanding the geology of eastern Canada.

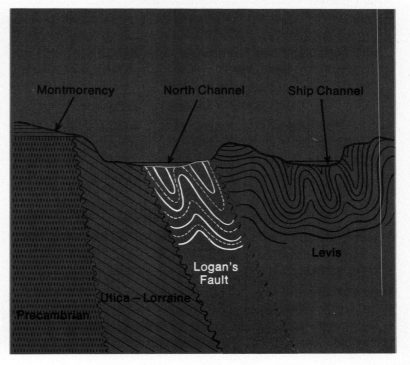

Logan's book, still a standard geological reference more than a century after he wrote it.

Closer observation of the fault, though, has worked less to confirm Logan's theory of its origin than to complicate it. Contemporary geologists distinguish among many different kinds of rock fault. They suspect that Logan's Fault incorporates several of these, and are now trying to define and interpret them one by one. Physically, much of the fault consists simply of broken, mixed rock, breccia, in a belt seldom more than a few hundred feet wide. Zones of this kind show themselves clearly where Logan's Fault crosses the Bescancour and Nicolet Rivers, and again where it dips into the Saint Lawrence.

The fault appears in a more dramatic form at Philipsburg, fifty miles south of Montreal. Here, above the beach of Lake Champlain at the southern end of the town, there is a path along the base of a short cliff. The path leads to a sheared rock face, marked by giant flutings, that strikes due northeast from the beach. Crushed, highly deformed shales press against the rock face. This is a major fault of the kind called a thrust fault. From the Philipsburg thrust fault and various other indications, there seems to be emerging among geologists a measure of agreement about a new theory of early rock movements in the region. Even before the first Appalachian ranges began to rise, according to this theory, a hugh block of sedimentary rock slid by the force of gravity northwest to collide with the Canadian Shield. Logan's Fault would then mark the frontier zone where the sliding rock mass—larger than the Maritime peninsula—was stopped by the rooted mass of the Shield. If this were so, Logan's Fault would probably extend from the Saint Lawrence estuary, where physical surveying instruments now lose touch with it, across the continental shelf to the ocean basin. In that case, shock-wave and gravity measurements should indicate a sudden change of density in the rock formations below the Cabot Strait. Although very few such surveys have so far been made, and these in less than adequate detail, they tend to confirm the presence of a major fault on the floor of the continental shelf.

Whether or not this array of evidence is conclusive, most reports on the Saint Lawrence Submarine Valley now assume that the underwater trough follows a line of separation between important units of the earth's crust. One such report, describing samples of sediment recovered from the valley's floor, says simply that "the location of the valley is tectonically controlled." Controlled, that is, by a frontier between moveable masses of rock. The authors of this particular report, D. J. G. Nota and D. H. Loring, were primarily interested in accounting for the contours of the submarine valley. From the bottom samples they recovered, and Dr. Nota's highly developed knowledge of comparable submarine troughs in other parts of the world, they concluded that the history of the Saint Lawrence submarine valley was probably governed by these events: (1) River erosion along the fault zone described above. The rivers, there might have been several, would have been ancestral stages of the Saint Lawrence, running all the way across the continental shelf during periods when the sea was low and the land high. At these times what is now the bottom of the Gulf of Saint Lawrence was a coastal plain extending from the Maritime peninsula to the slope of the continental shelf. (2) Glacial erosion widening and deepening the former river bed. The ice lobe would have crossed the full width of the continental shelf, and probably scoured the trough clean of sediment and loose rock. (3) Some filling and smoothing of the raw post-glacial contours by silt washed into the trough during the last few thousand years. At its deepest, this new layer of sediment seems to be nowhere much more than seventy feet thick. Most of the layer is composed of crystalline particles eroded from the Canadian Shield; for some reason, the Appalachian rocks south of the Saint Lawrence apparently shed very little sediment toward the river.

Should this turn out to be an accurate summary of the trough's history, the submarine valley of the Saint Lawrence will be defined as an important but local feature of the earth's crust. Two McGill geologists, however, have proposed an alternate history with global implications. Each of the ocean basins is divided by a ridge higher and broader than most mountain ranges. The mid-Atlantic Ridge has recently been studied fairly closely, and scientists of the Lamont Oceanographic Laboratories have interpreted their measurements to reveal, surprisingly, a deep trough along the summit of the ridge. Apparently the ridge has been split by a double fault along its full length, allowing the wedge of rock left between the faults to sink deeper into the crustal layer below. The huge, shear-walled depression left along the top of the ridge by the sinking wedge is called by geologists a rift valley.

Many geologists now believe the mid-Atlantic rift to be part of a global web of similar double faults in the earth's crust— master faults, as it were, that divide the crust into moveable sections of super-continental size. Such a rift, according to P. S. Kumarapeli and V. A. Saull of McGill, may well branch from the mid-Atlantic rift near the Azore Islands, and follow an identified ridge (known as the southeast Newfoundland ridge) to the continental shelf. Here, if this should be the case, the rift acquires a name: the Saint Lawrence Submarine Valley. Emerging on the continent, the rift then becomes the surface Saint Lawrence Valley and, continuing west, the Ottawa Valley. Along traces of similar faults the rift just may advance through the Lake Superior basin, bend to the southwest, and eventually reach Texas.

The authors found most of their reasons for bringing forward this ambitious theory in a close study of the structural details of the Saint Lawrence Valley and its submarine extension. The stone walls of the valley, they say, rise in many places as though sheared by the kind of double fault that characterizes rift valleys in other parts of the world. The dimensions of both the surface and submarine valleys are consistent with those of rift valleys elsewhere. So is the pattern of subsidiary thrust faults in the Saint Lawrence Valley floor. (With the possible exception of Logan's Fault; "its precise nature is in doubt," the geologists say.) Volcanic intrusions often appear in rift valleys, so that the Monteregian Hills, otherwise a mystery, are a predictable part of the landscape if the Saint Lawrence is a rift valley. Finally, the theory that this is a rift valley might account for the least familiar but most violent aspect of the valley's behaviour. Earthquakes are often associated with rift valleys. In the valley of the Saint Lawrence and Ottawa River they happen far more often than most of the people who live there suppose.

"Some mountains were engulfed and disappeared," wrote a citizen of Quebec in 1663. "Waterfalls are levelled and many rivers are no more. The ground cracked and opened crevices of unmeasured depth. And there has resulted such a disorder of fallen and splintered trees that one sees today fields of more than a thousand arpents all levelled as if they had been recently tilled, in many places where there was nothing but forest." The earth-

quake he was describing had taken place in February of that year near the mouth of the Saguenay River, well over a hundred miles from Quebec. Farther away still, in the New England states, the same tremors were said to have caused a widespread religious revival.

Interpreting these and other contemporary accounts, seismic experts estimate that the Saguenay earthquake was roughly comparable in magnitude to the one that destroyed San Francisco. Since then there have been at least thirteen more earthquakes of damaging magnitude at various points in the Saint Lawrence Valley, and several more in the tributary valley of the Ottawa. During the 1960's an average of five earthquakes a year, some very slight, have been recorded in the Saint Lawrence and Ottawa Valleys. In most cases their focal points have been about ten miles deep in the crust.

All these measurements, besides establishing the Saint Lawrence Valley among the high earthquake-risk zones of the world, are consistent with the theory that the Saint Lawrence may be a rift valley. For the present this theory has the scientific status of an interesting guess, not much more; but it fits a pattern of thought that seems likely to dominate geological ideas for some time to come. This is an attempt to understand the earth less as a collection of rocks than as a system of harmonics, a variable field in which continents drift and rigid stone "flows" in changeable currents, a tuned movement as constant and as inconstant as, to a man looking out from Quebec Rock, the river seems in its passage to the sea.

A last geological measurement may help connect the rock and water of the valley with this kinetic view of the globe. In 1926 a small network of fixed points was set up near Quebec City to investigate the bizarre possibility that the banks of the river were moving. A check of the network in 1964 detected no movement. The next year a far more elaborate network was established, covering both sides of the river for almost a hundred miles. The new network included several points fixed in 1926. This time, the check for movement during the intervening fifty years was inconclusive; there is an indication that the banks of the river have moved past each other by two or three feet. All great rivers run eventually to the sea; in the case of the Saint Lawrence, it seems that the riverbank may be running in the same direction.

THE AQUATIC ENVIRONMENT

The St. Lawrence River dominates the natural environment of the valley and acts as a north-south dividing line for those species unable to cross the river. The area also provides an excellent environment for many species of plants and animals which are just beginning to colonize the region. However man's alteration of the river has resulted in an alteration of the vast profusion of plant and animal life that depends on the river for survival. The long-nosed gar, (above) can breathe without using its gills by utilizing its swim bladder as a lung in an emergency, it can frequently be seen at the surface of the river gulping air.

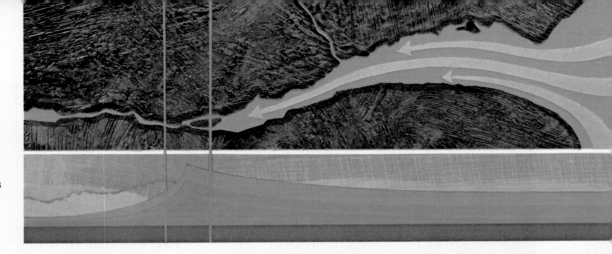

The brackish zone

The currents and tides in the estuary cause a mixing of the salt-water carried in by the tide and the fresh water brought down the river by the currents. The area of the estuary where the salt and fresh water meet and mix is called the brackish zone. Although it may be considered a transitional area, it has its own community of life forms, many of which face a unique problem – they must be able to live in both salt and fresh water. Thus their bodies must be able to evacuate the excess salt when they are in the ocean, yet be able to exist without any salt at all in the fresh water river. Plant forms found in this zone are phytoplankton, algae, seaweeds and eelgrasses. Some of the few animal species able to exist in this area are: 1. sea trout 2. lamprey 3. stickleback 4. sandworm 5. cancer crab 6. American eel and 7. shrimp.

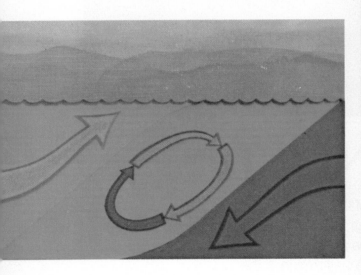

The arrows (above) signify how the water temperature can change. Warm, fresh water of the current initially remains on top, and much colder salt-water from the tidal inflow goes to the bottom. Gradually a mean temperature is reached between the two extremes.

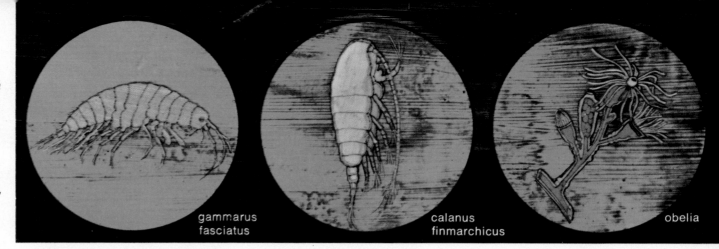

◄ The brackish zone occupies the area between the two lines – the point at which the fresh water current meets the inward-moving salt-water tide.

► The gammarus fasciatus, a prolific amphipod, the calanus finmarchicus, a crustacean about the size of a rice-grain, and the polyp, obelia, are small animals washed into the brackish zone with each wave.

gammarus fasciatus

calanus finmarchicus

obelia

Adaptations
to the current

1. *Cladophora* may be anchored to rocks with hairlike filaments which trail downstream. Despite their minuscule size, they are so abundant they often colour the water with greenish-grey scum.

2. The larvae of the net-veined midge survive well in rapids and waterfalls, affixing themselves to rocks. This quarter-inch-long larva crawls from rock to rock, scraping plants from their surfaces.

3. Caddisfly larvae construct half-inch turtle-shaped cases out of sand grains and tiny pebbles which they later fasten to current-washed rocks where they remain until the larvae emerge as adults.

4. Stone-fly nymphs live in the water for a year before taking to the air. Adults can usually be found attached to leaves on streamside trees. When at rest, they fold their wings back over their bodies.

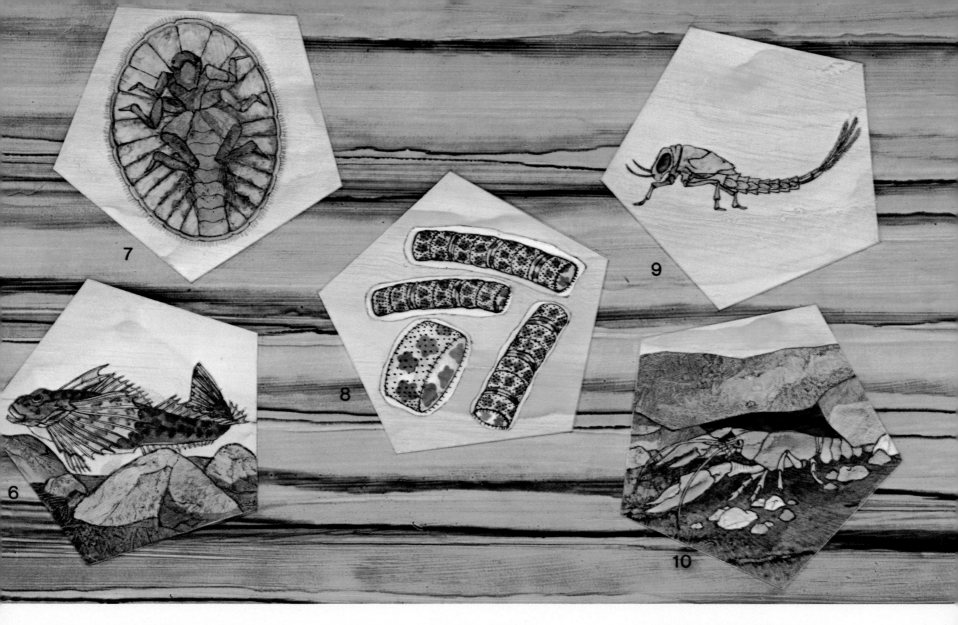

5. Half-inch-long black-fly larvae utilize their fan-like heads to comb food particles from the current. If a larva loses its grip, a silken lifeline restrains it from being carried away by the current.

6. The mottled sculpin, a large-headed, six-inch-long fish, frequently found in cold, upland streams, defies the current's pull by spreading its forefins against the upstream side of river stones.

7. Water pennies are flattened, oval-shaped beetle larvae that cling to rocks. Their heads, legs and gills are visible only when the larvae are scraped off the stones on the river bottom.

8. The *melosira,* a microscopic algae commonly found in the St. Lawrence, can be particularly troublesome since it has a tendency to clog filters at water purification plants in the river.

9. Clinging to a stone, the mayfly nymph, *isonychia,* spreads out its bristly front legs to catch flowing food particles. Most mayfly nymphs graze on some form of algae that grow in fresh water.

10. The crayfish avoids the current by sheltering beneath rocks and stones on the stream bottom. Normally, it uses legs for locomotion, as it crawls suspiciously from place to place.

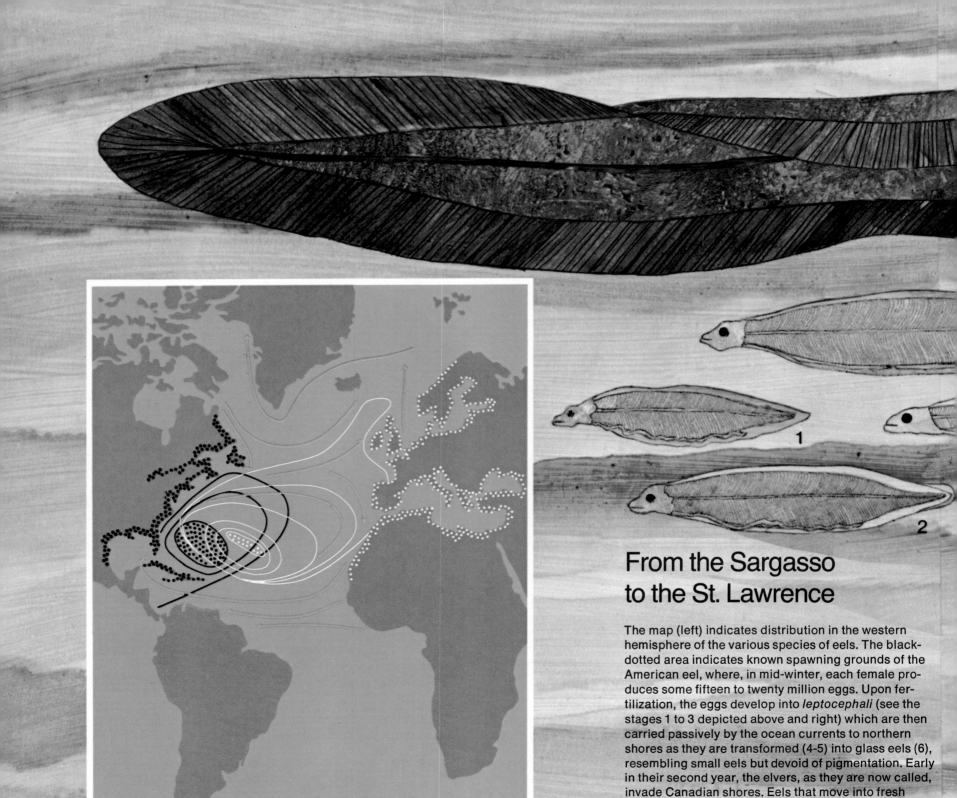

From the Sargasso to the St. Lawrence

The map (left) indicates distribution in the western hemisphere of the various species of eels. The black-dotted area indicates known spawning grounds of the American eel, where, in mid-winter, each female produces some fifteen to twenty million eggs. Upon fertilization, the eggs develop into *leptocephali* (see the stages 1 to 3 depicted above and right) which are then carried passively by the ocean currents to northern shores as they are transformed (4-5) into glass eels (6), resembling small eels but devoid of pigmentation. Early in their second year, the elvers, as they are now called, invade Canadian shores. Eels that move into fresh water develop slowly but exist there for up to ten years.

The American eel is an elongate and serpentine animal with a pointed head and numerous needle-like teeth in its jaw. Possessing single, small gill openings on each side just in front of the pectoral fins, the eel lacks pelvic fins and its caudal, dorsal and anal fins are combined in one long fin extending down the entire body.

3

5

4

6

7

The preservation of the Ouananiche

Despite the long isolation the ouananiche has enjoyed apart from the mainstream of Atlantic salmon, its classification as a distinct sub-species has no justification on any genetic grounds, and the ouananiche has come to be regarded as just another alternative name for the Atlantic salmon. Construction of dams, mills, deforestation, pollution and other agricultural activities for some time rendered the future of the ouananiche, as well as other fish, in serious jeopardy. In recent times, hatcheries have been instrumental in re-establishing numbers and providing clear water and danger-free breeding grounds for the ouananiche.

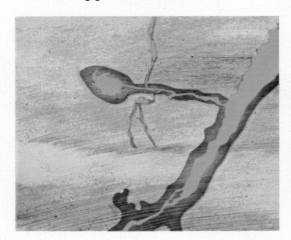

Legend has it that thousands of years ago, when the Wisconsin glacial waters finally receded from the St. Lawrence valley, some Atlantic salmon were unable to return to the Atlantic Ocean, and became trapped in Lake St. John and various other northern lakes in eastern Quebec. These fish were called *aonanch* (land-locked) by the Lake St. John Montagnais. Since that time, the ouananiche has become one of the best loved sporting fishes in North America.

The female adult ouananiche is "stripped" of eggs; the average number of eggs produced by each female is approximately two thousand.

The male's milt is "stripped" to fertilize female eggs; some males are sexually mature when they are ten inches long.

The fertilized eggs are laid in clear water on top of a matting of gravel and small pebbles at the bottom of a shallow, sunlit stream.

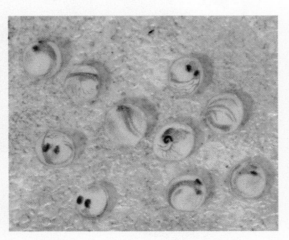

Newly-hatched eggs, or alevins, resemble pink-ish eye-balls, and possess a yolk sac which provides all the necessary nourishment.

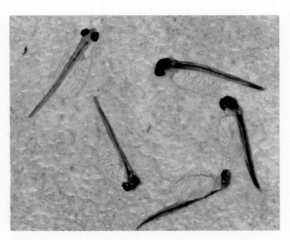

The young fingerlings feed almost exclusively on insects, though they also favour immature aquatic animals and newly-laid trout eggs.

A migrant from the south

Born in a litter of twenty to twenty-five (1) only two weeks after parental mating, the baby opossum (2) arrives blind, deaf, hairless and so minute that two dozen of them barely fill a teaspoon. Each baby (3) weighs less than an ounce. The newly born opossum immediately finds its way to the mother's pouch, crawling the two or three inches up the female's fur on its tiny forelegs which are developed (4) out of all proportion to the rest of its embryonic body. Even inside the pouch, the struggle for survival continues; the usual number of teats on the North American opossum, thirteen—nine is the minimum, seventeen the maximum—is not sufficient to nurse her average brood of twenty. While some perish of starvation, the lucky baby opossums (5) hang onto the nipples for two months until they are fully developed, pressing the teat against the roofs of their mouths with their powerful tongues. As the adult male is totally disinterested in his mate and brood, the female herself must go out in the country and forage for food as well as protect her young. Gradually and tentatively baby opossums emerge from the pouch (6); at first, they ride on top of their mother, and, later, when they are fifteen weeks old, they are ready to make the break and venture into the open land alone. The opossum's struggle is by no means over. An omnivorous eater of both animals and grains, seeds and fruit, the opossum is also prey to man and other carnivorous animals against which it offers only a meagre defence. Though its life expectancy is short, many of the opossum's inadequacies are compensated for by additional advantages; the animal's remarkable fecundity alone has not saved it from extinction. The opossum is a night creature, burrowing by day in secluded cavities. Furthermore, it is an excellent climber, clambering up trees on its nail-less, grasping hind toes, and resting on branches by its scaly, prehensile tail. The opossum also possesses fifty sharp little teeth (7) —more than that of any other North American mammal—and very well developed front paws (8).

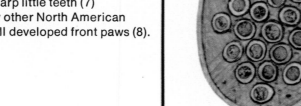

1

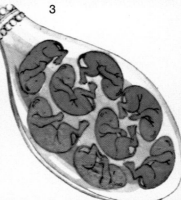

2

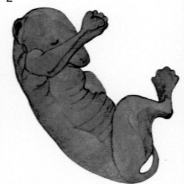

3

4   5   6   7   8

PART THREE / **PLANT LIFE**

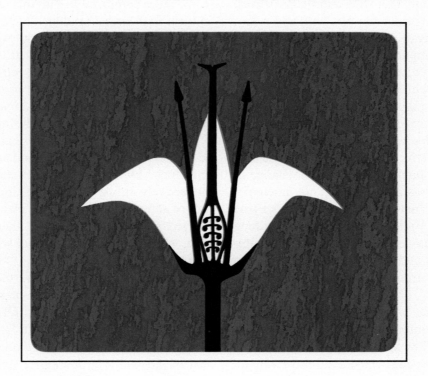

6 MIGRANTS AND COLONIZERS

Fleabane, a many-flowered herb with a yellow disk and white, pink or purple rays, grows in one variety or another over much of the earth; of more than a dozen North American varieties one, the Philadelphian, has been found from Newfoundland to British Columbia, from Labrador to Texas; but an extreme form of Philadelphian fleabane, with a smoother stem and slicker leaves, has been found only on a slate cornice ten feet long and a foot wide near the shore of Bellechasse Bay, in the estuary of the Saint Lawrence not far downstream from the Isle d'Orleans. Tidewater sprays the cornice but rarely submerges it. It is just another wet rock on a long shoreline.

The singular bed of fleabane illuminates the plant life of the Saint Lawrence Valley in several ways, the most striking of which, perhaps, is negative. Almost alone among several hundred kinds of plants that grow in the region, the Bellechasse fleabane has adapted to life in this habitat by a physical change of form, from a small hairy plant to a glabrous one; not much of a change, but a unique one. In this new form, the fleabane is a true native of the Saint Lawrence Valley. Most of the remaining plants of the valley are not natives. They are unchanged migrants, typical of other regions, and they characterize the Saint Lawrence Valley only by their frequency and the associations they form here.

But if the Bellechasse fleabane has made a special adaptation to life on the Saint Lawrence estuary, why is it a prisoner on a wet shelf of rock ten feet long? The answer is unknown. But the question leads directly to the broader consideration of why all the plants of the valley, or indeed any other region, grow where they do. Until the present generation of botanists, the theoretical assumption was the same one suggested to most people by common sense; plants seek first the climate, and then the soil, where they will grow best. Do climate and soil, then, control not only the growth of plants but their distribution? Most botanists now suspect that common sense may, in this case, have been misleading their colleagues for several generations.

What does control the pattern of plant life? Chance, mainly; or so it begins to seem. "The conclusion is that the ranges of plants frequently reflect a chance history of migration related to the vagaries of opportunity, competition, and disturbances such as fire," according to Dr. J. S. Rowe, a Canadian scientist whose special study is tree biology. Dr. Rowe speaks of the "haphazard groupings" that result from "the continuing, dynamic evolution and migration of plants. Therefore," he concludes, "it is a mistake to look for close relationships between plant distributions and climate or soils."

With time to get used to the idea, common sense may become more comfortable with this understanding of a plant world subject to the same random effects we see at work in the human worlds than with the old view of an order logically predetermined by climate and soil. What is happening, it seems, is that biologists are making the same retreat from certainty that geologists were seen to be making in the previous chapter; and as their science becomes less axiomatic it becomes more subtle, more interesting, and more believable.

It also becomes more historical, since the random events that led some plants to one place and some to another were strongly influenced by where the plants started from, and when. In the attractively simple case of the Saint Lawrence Valley, there is no doubt about when most of the plants that now mantle the valley started the migration that led them here: ten thousand years ago, when the last ice sheet had withdrawn and the Champlain Sea was beginning to recede.

The retreating ice cap and the ebbing flood left behind a bald, raw landscape; for non-marine plant life, it was an uncolonized world, a beginning. Of the previous beginning, the origin of life on earth, God (still) only knows the full story, although some scientists are beginning to think they may learn a few of the details in the rearrangement of crystals among molecules of wet clay, while others are seeking them among molecular colonies on the surface film of the ocean. Wherever plant life began, several full spectra of plant orders came and went in the Saint Lawrence Valley during the few billion years that followed, including such exotic tropical excesses as huge palms and ferns. Toward the end of the Mesozoic Era, not much more than a hundred million years ago, there was a great expansion of temperate climate, including Canada's. Derivatives of the earlier tropical plants adapted to the cooling environment during the next fifty million years. By the beginning of the Tertiary period, between fifty and sixty million years ago, most of the plant elements were present in Canada that are present now. So much is "fairly clear" to contemporary botanists; not many would claim to be able to trace this evolution in finer detail.

Fossil relics of these ancestral plant forms are relatively scarce in the Saint Lawrence Valley. Some of these same plants grow in the valley now, but they are generally considered to be migrants that reinvaded the lowlands after the ice withdrew from the bald surface.

A generation ago, most botanists thought that one group of plants must have managed to live through the ice age without being wiped out in the Saint Lawrence region. Plant collectors, among them the most affectionately remembered of all early Canadian botanists, frère Marie-Victorin, had discovered a large number of alpine or arctic plants growing in small clusters on the Gaspé Peninsula. They were all related to plants that grow in the high Rockies, the high Arctic or Siberia, but none had even been found growing south of Gaspé, or between Gaspé and the western mountains. To account for their presence on the Saint Lawrence, the leading American botanist of the day, M. L. Fernald, of Harvard, set out the Nunatak theory.

The phrase sounds congenially Canadian, and the theory still appears in many Canadian textbooks. Nunatak is the Eskimo word for a high rock formation that projects through a surrounding ice sheet—an island in a glacier. Briefly, Fernald's Nunatak theory held that the arctic plants on the Gaspé Peninsula were ancient inhabitants of the Shickshock Mountains there. During the ice ages they survived on the upper ridges of the mountains, which projected above the ice as nunataks. When the last ice sheet withdrew, these "relics" were already "too old and conservative to pioneer" on the bald ground uncovered by the ice. They stayed where the botanists found them.

By the 1930's, according to the curator of the Montreal Botanical Gardens, Marcel Raymond, "the so-called Nunatak theory reigned supreme among most northeastern American botanists." But if the theory solved one problem for botanists, it raised a more serious problem for many geologists. They had long concluded that the last ice sheet must have been about two miles deep—which was absurd if numberless ridges of the Shickshock Mountains, none much more than four thousand feet high, had projected through the ice as nunataks.

Who was right? The geologists, probably; at least most geologists and botanists now agree that most of the evidence discovered since the 1930's suggests that the ice sheet was indeed two miles deep. Moreover, they now feel that the random events of migration and competition account quite adequately for the movement of the troublesome alpine plants from unglaciated sanctuaries in the far Arctic and on the Labrador coast to their outposts on the Gaspé Peninsula. Almost as though Fernald's description of these plants as "too old and conservative to pioneer" had been a deliberate insult, contemporary writers leap to the defense. "For the present," says V. C. Wynne-Edwards, "the details of where the Arctic-alpine flora weathered out the Wisconsin (glacial) period can rest, provided the facts are established that it did not do so upon nunataks well within the glaciated area, and that it is not a relict flora afflicted with pioneering inefficiency, but one vigorous in adaptation to the conditions it finds, distributed essentially by post-Wisconsin migration."

There has never been any controversy, even of this mild and attractive quality, over where the rest of the plants now found in the Saint Lawrence Valley weathered the ice ages. They retreated to what botanists call refugia south of the ice front, mainly in the United States. Just where in the south any particular species found a refuge is less certain. White spruce and tamarack fossils have been found below the Mason-Dixon line, eight hundred miles south of the most southerly specimens now growing naturally. Birch and pine seem to have weathered the glaciers farther north, in the American Appalachians, although they now tend to concentrate south of the heaviest stands of white spruce and tamarack.

Some plant forms that grew in the Saint Lawrence region where the ice came may have been unequal to the slow adaptive movement south, and perished altogether. Some of the plants that followed the retreating ice sheet north and colonized the nude valley may never have grown there before; there seems no way to tell. What is certain is that nearly all the present forms of plant life natural to the valley migrated here from the south during the last ten thousand years: mosses, ferns, herbs, wildflowers, grasses, tubers, creepers, bushes, vines, and trees. The species with light seeds borne on the wind or the water were the first to move into the new ground. Those with heavier seeds followed more slowly in the cycle of migration.

THE STRUCTURE OF A PLANT CELL

*All plants and animals are composed of
minute units of living matter called
cells. All the vital activities that go
on in an organism are performed by cells
which vary in complexity depending
on their function. The simplest
living organisms are unicellular,
consisting of just one cell. All cells
are basically divided into two parts –
the nucleus, or control centre, and the
cytoplasm, a thick liquid which
surrounds all other elements in the
cell. In new cells the cell wall (1)
is composed primarily of pectin and is
quite flexible. The walls become thicker
and more inflexible as the cell matures.
The nucleus (2) is the most important
section of the cell, it contains the
DNA and RNA which determine what the
plant will be and then control all cell
functions. Energy for the cell is provided by the mitochondria (3) which contains proteins and converts the food
to a state usable by the plant.
Essential in photosynthesis the chloroplasts
(4) contain green pigment which absorbs
the sun's energy and converts carbon
dioxide into sugar. The plant colour is
determined by carotene chromoplasts
(5) but the exact function of the golgi
structures (6), which may act as a
chemical storehouse, remains a mystery.
A network of passages between membranes,
the endoplasmic reticulum (7), provides
a means for the transfer of material
within the cell. Plants maintain their
reserve supply of food in tiny layers
of carbohydrates called starch grains
(8). The combination of these elements
are responsible for the miracle of life.*

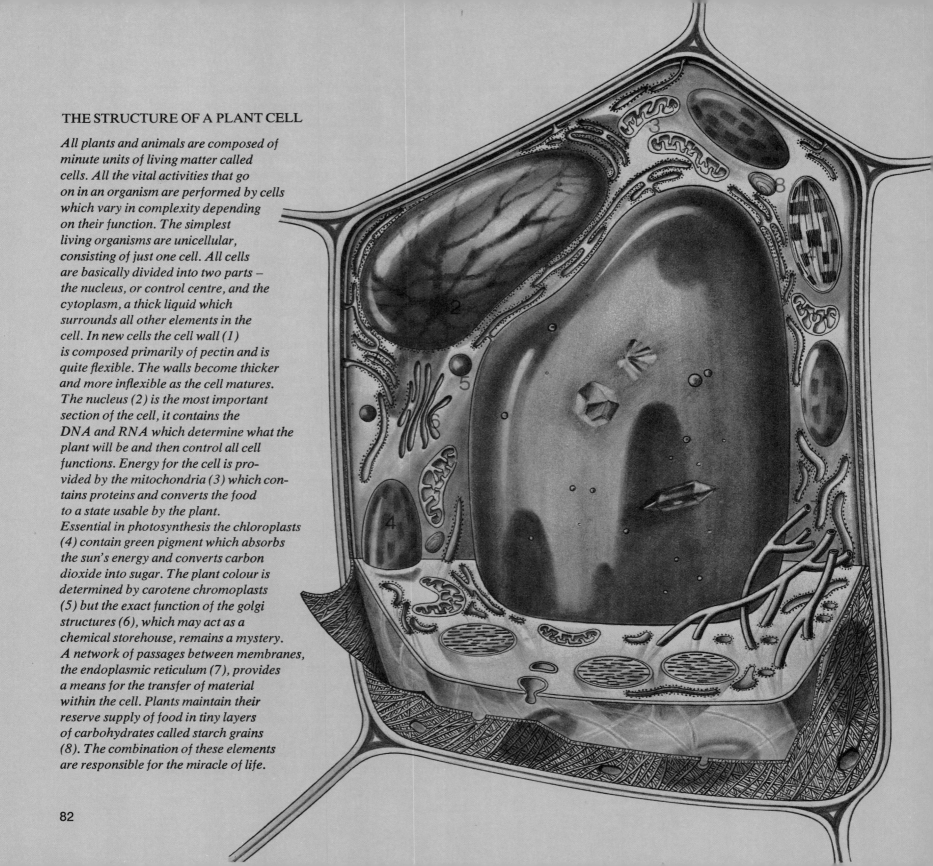

82

Near Quebec City, in the slate uplands to the north and east, the texture of the landscape is improved by an abundance of natural meadows. Peter Kalm, the Swedish botanist who explored this terrain in 1749, found them one of the main pleasures of the countryside. "The further I advanced northward here the finer were the meadows," he said, "and the turf upon them was better and closer." The turf he identified as a mixture of two plants: "At the root of the meadow grass the ground is covered with white clover, so that one cannot wish for finer meadows than are found here. Almost all have been formerly tilled fields, as appears from the furrows on the ground, which still remain."

The notion of widespread glaciation was still a century in the future, so that Kalm may be forgiven for supposing that glacial furrows had been ploughed by habitants. But a similar confusion probably still arises for most people who stand on the edge of a natural meadow fringed by trees growing thickly on poorer soil at the meadow's edge. Unless the meadow had been cleared by hand, wouldn't the trees have taken it over? The answer biologists now tend to give is: not necessarily. The right combination of ground plants, moving fast and reaching the meadow-to-be in advance of the first trees, could so mantle the ground that tree seeds would never get a foothold. The early arrival of such a combination of grasses would, of course, depend on chance—but, in this view, the meadows are there to show that these random events actually happened. "After all," says J. S. Rowe, the tree biologist quoted earlier, "the major factor in competition is getting there first, of (sic) pre-empting space in soil and air, and by that pre-emption excluding later arrivals."

The actual order in which returning plants reached the Saint Lawrence Valley after the ice age seems to have been closely examined only in the cases of the trees. A heavy forest dominated the plant life of the valley until we lopped it off. The "weeds" of the advancing tree-line were white spruce, black spruce, tamarack, birch, poplar and willow, all trees with light seeds, fast-moving migrants. Spruce now at the northern tree-line in the Keewatin District have marched a thousand miles

Angeosperms, the most advanced order in the plant kingdom, divide ▶ into two groups depending on the number of seed leaves in each seed.

PLANT STRUCTURE	Dicotyledons	Monocotyledons
The cotyledons, or seedling leaves, which are used for photosynthesis also give the plants their name. The dicots have two seedling leaves while the monocots have only one seed leaf.		
Leaves are primarily organs of photosynthesis adapted to expose a maximum amount of surface to the light and air. Dicot leaves tend to be deeply lobed. Monocots are parallel-veined.	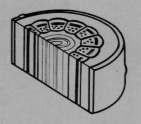	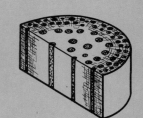
The plant stems serve two primary functions, they transport materials between the leaves and the roots and they serve as food storage organs. The dicot is formally structured.		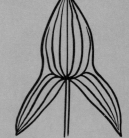
The roots act as both an anchor for the plant and as an organ of absorption for water and minerals. Some monocot plants produce bulbs for reproduction and food storage.		
Flowers are concerned with reproduction. Dicot flowers usually have their petals and sepals in groups of fours and fives. Monocot flowers are usually grouped in a multiple of three.		

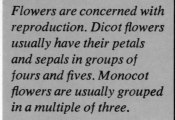

north in ten thousand years—a mile every ten years, three or four miles in every generation. Behind them came slower moving, larger-seeded trees: pines, maples, elms, basswood, small-fruited trees such as wild cherries and mountain ashes. Behind them, trees with large, heavy seeds, the oaks, hickories, walnut, butternut.

About fifty kinds of trees had reached the heart of the Saint Lawrence Valley by the beginning of the nineteenth century, when woodcutting changed from a chore to an industry and the forest was stripped. Here and there, though, individual stands of all fifty species survive, and biologists still speak of them as part of one of eight Canadian forest regions, the Great Lakes-Saint Lawrence Forest. This is a "mixed" forest; the forest takes its character from a mingling of evergreen and broad-leaved trees. The dominant evergreens, white pine and hemlock, are only slightly less conspicuous than the dominant hardwoods, sugar and red maples, yellow birch and beech. The territory, or "range," covered by this forest reaches from Lake of the Woods to New Brunswick, and in the Saint Lawrence region its northern and southern margins are roughly those of the lowlands themselves. But the Great Lakes-Saint Lawrence Forest described here is largely a statistical abstraction, an averaging exercise that has more reality on an index map than on the floor of the forest, where any rock may be surrounded by an entirely different mesh of trees.

Foresters, accordingly, have subdivided the forest into sections, several of them in the Saint Lawrence Valley alone. The reach of the Saint Lawrence described in Part One as the

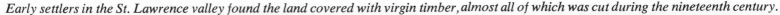
Early settlers in the St. Lawrence valley found the land covered with virgin timber, almost all of which was cut during the nineteenth century.

high river, flowing across the Frontenac Axis from Lake Ontario and dropping through the Ottawa-Saint Lawrence lowlands to the floor of the valley near Montreal, corresponds fairly closely to the area assigned on the range maps to the Upper Saint Lawrence Section of the forest. Hardwoods set the character of the woods; sugar maple and beech dominate a close weave of trees that includes yellow birch, white elm, red maple, basswood, white ash, red, white and bur oak and large-toothed aspen, with here and there a stand of rock elm or blue beech.

Along the Saint Lawrence, down the southern tributaries and some distance up the Ottawa to the north, the riverbanks are edged in places by clusters of more decorative trees, butternut, cottonwood, slippery elm. Some evergreens appear in the weave like patches of a pricklier texture; hemlock, white spruce, some white pine, pitch pine on and near the Thousand Islands; and in swampy hollows tamarack, eastern white cedar, black spruce or black ash. Where fire has razed a clearing, large-toothed aspen and white birch usually reinvade the ground with white spruce and balsam fir close behind. Dense vegetation covers the forest floor, picked out in bright colours for a few weeks every year by a rich growth of spring-flowering ground plants: trilliums, violets, hepaticas, bloodroots, jack-in-the-pulpits. Where the forest opens a little, and on the fringes of the fields, the ground is often trimmed with ferns, among them rattlesnake ferns, oak ferns and weedy bracken, with an occasional spray of rare maidenhair fern. Rarer species carpet the peat bogs: Labrador tea, lambskill, liverworts, orchids. The forest feels and looks like a place where the sap rises swift and high.

East of a frontier roughly drawn by the Ottawa and Richelieu Valleys, the range-maps assign the tree cover of the lowlands to a different forest, the Lower Saint Lawrence Section. Sugar maple is still one of the dominant trees, usually associated with yellow birch, but two evergreens, hemlock and white pine, are also dominant trees here. Theoretically, at least, this is the most thoroughly mixed section of the entire mixed forest. Balsam fir, white birch and white spruce lace the woods along with silver maple, red oak, beech, white ash, some butternut, red pine, and white elm. Cottonwood and red maple are fairly common on the riverbanks, the swamps are dark with black ash, black spruce and cedar.

North of the Saint Lawrence, the limit of this section of the forest is drawn by the scarp of the Canadian Shield, where the granite wall encloses Quebec City and emerges on the foreshore. South of the river a new forest, the Eastern Townships Section, is assigned to the Appalachian foothills that begin to swell southwest of Quebec City and run south and east to the Vermont and New Hampshire borders. Here, on higher ground, the dominant trees are evergreens, white spruce and balsam fir. Although the forest growth is heavy, the number of species thins out; mainly sugar maple, yellow birch, white pine and hemlock on well-drained ground, cedar and black spruce in swampy patches, aspen and white birch in old fire-slashes.

Downstream from Quebec, the heavy mantle of trees on both sides of the Saint Lawrence estuary are not assigned to the Great Lakes-Saint Lawrence Forest at all. They appear on the range maps as part of the vast Boreal Forest, the predominantly evergreen, northern forest that covers the bulk of the Canadian land mass from Labrador to the Alaskan border. Two sections of the Boreal Forest touch on the Saint Lawrence. The Gaspé Section extends northeast along the higher ground of the Notre Dame and Shickshock Mountains from the Eastern Townships to the seaward cape of the Gaspé Peninsula. Black and white spruce are the dominant trees, large and well-developed where the soil is fairly deep, stunted in the swampy ground. White birch is laced among the spruces, and balsam fir is scattered over the lower slopes of the ridges. Where the ridges flatten to a foreshore plain, along much of the estuary's length, sugar maple, white pine and yellow birch follow the river, along with a few cottonwoods and red maples—much the same mixture, that is, that characterizes the Saint Lawrence forests farther upstream.

North across the estuary lies the northeastern coniferous section of the Boreal Forest, mantling the Canadian Shield from just below Quebec to the Gulf with a thick but uncomplicated cover dominated by balsam fir and black spruce. Among them grow smaller numbers of white spruce, white birch, aspen and balsam poplar, with a few stands of jack pine. There is a single break in the long march of this northern forest from Quebec to the sea. In a narrow corridor along the Saguenay, from the rivermouth on the Saint Lawrence north to Lake Saint John, the mixed forest of the upper Saint Lawrence reappears.

The life cycle of a mushroom

The surface of the mushroom gills is the portion where the spores are formed. Spores are produced by *basidia,* or spore-producing cells, that form the *humenium*, or covering layer on the surface of each gill. Usually, each *basidium* produces only four spores, though more have been recorded. The spores, which are individually minute (about 1/2,500th of an inch) shed downward from the cap until, on reaching full maturity, they are forcibly expelled from their point of attachment. Being heavier than air, the spores fall slowly and are often wind-borne. When a mushroom spore alights on soil favourable to growth, germination takes place. Each spore cell absorbs food through its cell-wall and then divides into two cells. Long chains of cells are formed which look to the undiscerning eye like threads. Each single thread is called a *hypha,* a tangle of threads a *mycelium*. In the soil the *mycelium* grows by nourishing itself on decaying vegetable matter. Then, at certain stages, the threads mat together to form little balls the size of pinheads. The pinheads grow larger to the size of shirt-buttons. Eventually, under the proper climatic conditions of warmth and moisture, the original tiny ball is transformed into the emergent fruiting body consisting of stem and cap. After a young button has emerged, it may elongate and expand to full maturity in a matter of hours or take as long as a week or two, depending on the species and the temperature. Normally, fruiting occurs once a year, in the autumn. Finally, when the mushroom has grown to its full size, the stem and cap resume the cycle as the reproductive agents of this fungus plant. The mushroom illustrated here is the *amanita muscaria* and is deadly poisonous.

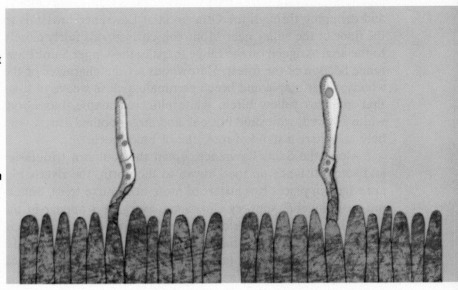

Basswood, white elm, black ash and balsam poplar line the banks; sugar maple, yellow birch, and white and red pine climb the slopes. In all but location, this is the forest of the warmer, richer valley floor far to the south. These, then, are the forests of the Saint Lawrence region, according to range maps and the statistical profiles of species. They are described here in some detail because in one dimension they are authentic and valuable; they tell how the heart of each of these forest sections is made up. But they have another dimension that is fictional and perhaps misleading; they divide the forests with hard, static borders, whereas on the ground the forest moves organically from one emphasis to another, more like a harmonic chord of mingled species than the wall of trees suggested by the range maps.

Not that the foresters who executed with great care the mapping of forests and sub-forests in Canada intended to propose a hard line at each border. They have been at pains to describe the overlap, the mingling of species at the margins. But the suspicion has been rising in the minds of some biologists that the range boundaries themselves, once they are mapped and published, may make it even harder to see the trees for the forest; the real trees, that is, for the forests outlined with such precision on paper. These paper forests, according to this view, feed our egocentric idea that the world we find ourselves standing in is the end product of natural history, that the way we see things is the way they are. Once we map the ranges of trees, the trees from then on seem to belong where we mapped them, and any deviations from these ranges seem to us somehow abnormal, unnatural.

But a tree, we are now being reminded by a few unsentimental biologists, belongs where it grows. Shagbark hickories standing on the Saint Lawrence are not misplaced strays from Florida but tough opportunists that have made a hard march

During the 1860's timber was a major item in Canada's foreign trade; it was brought by river to Quebec City for shipment to England.

north over hostile terrain, adapting with genetic brilliance to drastically shorter days and longer, harsher seasons of frost, competing for the ground they stand on with all the species that were there before them. Every tree in the Saint Lawrence Valley has much the same ancestral history, except of course, the cultivated trees and plants. They are all, at this moment, more or less well adapted to the soil and climate of the valley. More important, they are integrated with the chemical and biological functions of the so-called ecosystem around them—the web of active connections among earth, air and organic matter that sustains and balances life. They belong, for the moment, in the Saint Lawrence Valley. But they belong just as naturally anywhere else their vigour and competitive drive can take them.

Some of them will doubtless become the victims of tougher trees. Great white and red pines dominated much of the valley until the logging industry disposed of them at a profit during

Napoleon's blockade of the Baltic, and the avarice of the timber merchants has been much deplored. Still, there are convincing signs that the pines of the valley were in decline, yielding to the competition of more aggressive trees, before the first woodsmen swung an axe.

Other trees may equally well thrust north from the Saint Lawrence region to displace some of the species we are in the habit of saying "belong" in the high cold latitudes. Basswood, a particularly broad-leafed, southern-looking tree, took ten thousand years to reach the head of the Saguenay. Nobody knows where the most northerly basswood will stand in another ten thousand years. And that, surely, is what makes the forest interesting, even exciting, the sense that these trees are less a pattern of growth conforming to ranges of climate and soil than a collection of individuals competing in a natural arena for a place in the earth and the air.

The shagbark hickory and basswood are two southern trees which have slowly increased their range as far north as the St. Lawrence valley.

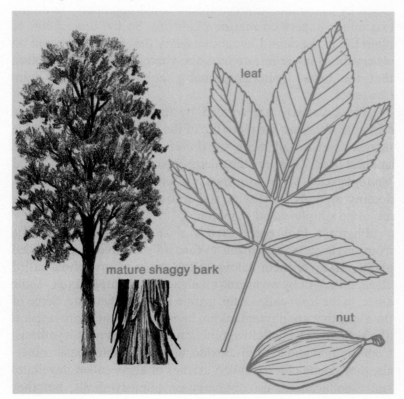

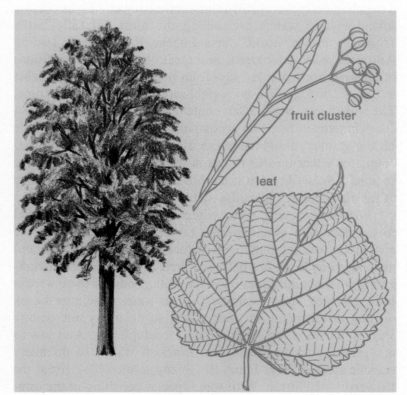

7 MARINE PLANT LIFE

The opening paragraph of this book described the Saint Lawrence as a river flowing between stone deserts. The river bottom, its margins and the water itself, on the other hand, might better be described as a desert's opposite.

In the Saint Lawrence estuary, the life zone made up of tidal water, the river bottom and banks, the mantle of air and the biochemical traffic among them all, is up to eight times more fertile than the moist forest of the Saint Lawrence Valley near the juncture with the Ottawa River. The estuary of the Saint Lawrence may well sustain a denser growth of life in a smaller area than any other Canadian environment between Gaspé and the Pacific Coast.

Although there seems to be an emerging consensus among biologists that this estimate of estuarine fertility is accurate, a twitch of controversy still animates the subject. "Estuaries and inland marine waters are among the most naturally fertile (regions) in the world," says Eugene P. Odum, a leading American marine biologist, in a recent book. "But conditions in estuaries are unstable," says John Bardach, another specialist in aquatic biology, in a book published at about the same time. "The wide fluctuations in salt content, as well as extreme differences in temperature that accompany tidal ebb and flow, make of the estuary a habitat more rigorous than would be encountered either upriver or out in the sea. Living in an estuary requires a versatility that is hard to reconcile with the tendency of all life processes toward a stable equilibrium."

For these reasons, most writers on marine life long tended to conclude that estuaries were rather barren places. But the conclusion was based more on deduction than observation, and as more knowledge has been acquired at first hand by investigating what actually goes on in the water, some of these writers have modified their opinions. "Just as water hyacinths die on drifting downstream into salt water, so do many microbiotic species. There is too short a time for adaptation. And just as mangroves push upstream into brackish water, so do many oceanic species," says James B. Lackey, a microbiologist at the University of Florida. With some species perishing in the estuary while others flourish, the balance, according to Professor Lackey, "reveals a large population . . . many species, and, for some species, many individuals." But other writers continue to insist that estuary conditions choke off the number of species. Estuarine plant life "tends to be abundant in total quantity, but limited as to the number of important species," says Gordon A. Riley, of the Bingham Oceanographic Laboratory.

The disagreement probably reveals more about the state of knowledge than about the variety of plant life in estuaries. Marine biology is a fairly new science, and an expensive one. Research at significant depths over meaningful periods of time has been compared to space research in a number of respects, including financial ones, and a factual account of estuarine life forms will probably take another generation of careful, demanding work. Longer, in Canada. The biologists cited above are all American only because there has been virtually no competent investigation of plant life in the Saint Lawrence estuary. The current government survey of the work done on the Atlantic Coast by Canadian oceanographers could apparently find only two minor papers on marine plant life. So the description of plant life in the Saint Lawrence estuary that follows is based on observations made in estuaries elsewhere, with the assumption that the broad patterns probably hold true for the Saint Lawrence.

These patterns are formed by the most elusive of living elements. Whereas the plant life of the land is dominated by the largest plants of all, trees, the dominant marine plants are the smallest ones. These are the microscopic organic particles called phytoplankton. The word means floating plants. Zooplankton, floating animals, drift with and feed on phytoplankton. Both are often simply called plankton.

Phytoplankton elude even a clear definition. They range from single-celled organisms to relatively complex, multi-celled plants. Many of them belong to the group of organisms called algae, although by no means all algae are phytoplankton—some algae, in the form called kelp, grow a hundred feet long. Some of the algae that are phytoplankton behave in one or more respects like animals. The definitive function of plants is photosynthesis; from sunlight and carbon-dioxide, along with some basic minerals, they create chlorophyll. Varieties of algae called flagellates and dinoflagellates usually carry on photosynthesis, but they also whip themselves through the water under their own power, and mobility is a definitive function of animals. Moreover, some flagellates and dinoflagellates do not carry on photosynthesis, and are therefore not phytoplankton. Other varieties of algae known as diatoms carry on photosynthesis but grow hard, siliceous shells, often in a strikingly elegant design of linked hexagons. Shell-growing is an animal characteristic, but these diatoms are phytoplankton, provided they drift freely in the water. Diatoms that put out stalks to attach themselves to the bottom or the shoreline are not phytoplankon. Similarly, some varieties of marine bacteria are phytoplankton, while others are not.

Phytoplankton in each of these general categories are presumably growing in the Saint Lawrence estuary, but in what numbers or varieties only much close study will tell. After several years of careful search, S. M. Conover, of the Bingham Oceanographic Laboratory, found 150 identifiable species of phytoplankton in Long Island Sound, and others too fragile to preserve. Less thorough searches made elsewhere have shown mainly that the kinds and numbers of phytoplankton in estuaries are endlessly variable. Whether any of them can survive only in this rigorous environment has yet to be learned. At least one authority, the microbiologist James B. Lackey, thinks this may be the case. "There are indications," he says, "that certain species may be found only in estuaries."

Other indications, as yet unexplored, suggest that the Saint Lawrence estuary may sustain phytoplankton in particularly large numbers. The deep submarine valley from the rim of the continental shelf to the upper estuary brings inshore a constant stream of fairly cold, very salty water rich in nutrient minerals. These are the conditions that lead in other estuaries to the largest crops of phytoplankton, but all three conditions rarely occur in the same estuary at the same time. They may make the waters of the Saint Lawrence estuary an almost ideal medium for growing phytoplankton. If so, this might account for a government report that there is twice as much plant life in the Saint Lawrence estuary as there is animal life.

Like the phytoplankton of the estuary, the floating plants of the upper, fresh-water reaches of the Saint Lawrence have been given very little serious attention. The general categories here are the same as the ones in the estuary; the particular species may vary widely, and probably do. Their role in the life cycle

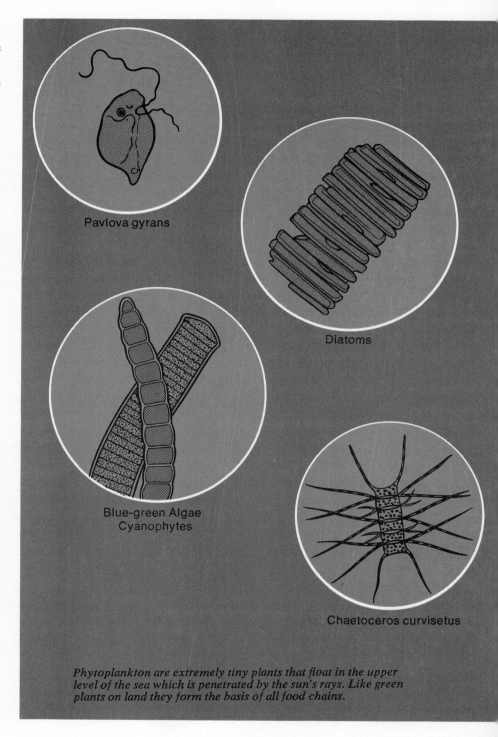

Pavlova gyrans

Diatoms

Blue-green Algae Cyanophytes

Chaetoceros curvisetus

Phytoplankton are extremely tiny plants that float in the upper level of the sea which is penetrated by the sun's rays. Like green plants on land they form the basis of all food chains.

Flowers of the marsh and the river shore

In contrast to the drier, more undulating land to the north, marshes are cool, moist habitats for most of the year. Many rare and beautiful plants thrive in the protection of this environment. The flowers on these pages are some of the hardiest plant forms in the wetlands of the valley.

The virginia water leaf is common in moist places throughout eastern North America.

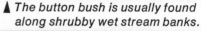

▲ The button bush is usually found along shrubby wet stream banks.

◄ The fleshy bulbs of the yellow pond lily were once cooked and eaten by Indians.

► The corolla of the square-stemmed monkey flower resembles the face of a monkey.

Attractive pickerelweed is occasionally of value as food for ducks and muskrats.

Touch-me-not derives its name from the seed pods which open at a touch.

▼ The roots of the delicate anemone can be eaten as potatoes and are high in starch.

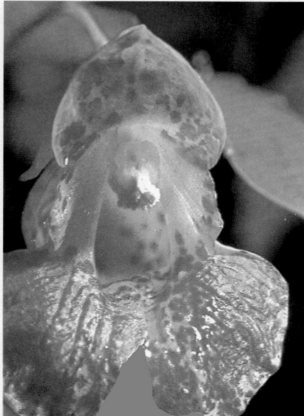

Nature's beautiful bounty

Ferns are some of the oldest forms of plant life and were found in great abundance some two hundred million years ago. Remains of these huge plants provide many of our most valuable coal deposits. Although today they are neither as plentiful nor as large, ferns are still found in most moist ground that is heavily shaded. Frequently they provide the only green floor cover in particularly dense stands of trees. As well as things of beauty they provide valuable humus and oxygen in the natural environment. The water lily is one of the most attractive pond flowers to both man and animals. The underside of its broad leaves provides a home for many tiny pond animals. Its rootstalk was a favourite food of the moose and it is frequently covered with insects seeking pollen.

Each morning the white water lily opens its petals to the sun's rays. ▶

Ferns provide a lush green carpet in the deep forest shade.

94

though, is the same in both parts of the river.

The phytoplankton are the green pastures of the water. Although, unlike land plants, they are green only in some cases; in others they are blue-green, yellow-green, golden-brown, brown, and red. They stain the water accordingly, at the not infrequent times when there is a population explosion, or "bloom", of one variety or another. The phytoplankton do the biological work that is done on land by the full spectrum of the plant kingdom, converting sunlight and chemicals to organic matter and setting oxygen free in the process. They feed on light energy, while most of the animals and not a few parasitic plants of the water feed ultimately on them. They are immeasurably the most important living element in the water.

They are also an almost direct link between contemporary life and life in its original form. From the first animated cluster of molecules to the single cell of simple algae cannot have been a great leap. The oldest algal fossil so far discovered was imprinted on chert in Ontario about one and a half billion years ago, and seems to differ little from algae growing in the Saint Lawrence at this moment. For how many millions or billions of years the same kind of algae had been drifting around before that particular fossil was formed will probably never be known. But the simple algae, and to a lesser extent most of the other forms of phytoplankton, clearly stand aloof from the evolutionary adventures that have given later, more complicated forms of life so much variety on the trip to extinction. Or do the algae stand above such adventures? If survival is the purpose of evolution, as we are assured it is, then the algae have out-evolved everything by not evolving.

In any case, among the phytoplankton the plant life of the river has no evolutionary history; they live in a permanent, eventless present. The evolutionary history of all but a handful of other water plants is almost equally placid. Many one-celled varieties of fungus, among them several strains of yeast, float among the phytoplankton, living parasitically but successfully. On the bottom of the estuary, and on the apparently barren flats of mud that dry at low tide, grow those diatoms that have learned to anchor themselves by putting out stalk-like tubes. At times, usually in early spring or late fall, the diatoms flower prodigiously, and then they come to outnumber all the other microflora of the estuary.

The first *visible* form of plant life in the estuary is kelp, the long, brown chains of algal cells known simply as seaweed. Here and there the surface is splotched with clusters of green algal cells, arranged in a pattern that has earned them the name sea lettuce. Both kinds of algae are salt-water plants; they disappear upstream as fresh water dilutes the tidal stream. Next, along either shore, a few mosses and ferns appear, fresh-water forms that have pressed downstream, adapting to the saltier environment as they advanced.

In the offshore shallows, a new order of plants has appeared, the first representatives of several upriver species. These plants reproduce by generating pollen or seeds, like most land plants. They are thought, indeed, to be the survivors of an evolutionary junket in which they adapted from life in the water to life on land and then made all but the final stage of the return trip. The hero of this adventure is a pondweed called eelgrass. On the return leg, most of the other plants stopped when they touched salt water. Eelgrass moved on through the estuaries, adapting to higher concentrations of salt as it went, until now it grows in shallows wherever the Atlantic coast is sheltered from the open sea. Quebec's phrase for it is *mousse de mer,* sea foam.

A single blade of eelgrass supports a vast community of microscopic life. Diatoms and tiny worms attach themselves to each new blade (1) and quickly increase to the point where they obscure the outline of the blade (2). This wealth of prey attracts amphipods (3) and other predators.

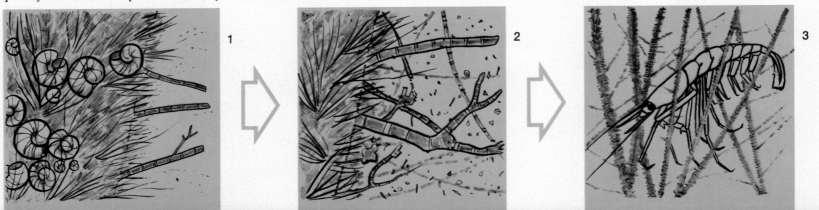

Pale green, stirred constantly by the water, meadows of eelgrass grow in the tidal shallows between the shore and the deep channels of the Saint Lawrence estuary. Each plant is rooted in the mud. From a fleshy tuber, rich in starch, it puts up slender, creeping blades that lie on the surface at low tide and disappear below the water as the tide rises.

The eelgrass meadows are easy to overlook altogether. They are more common along the sometimes low slope on the south shore of the estuary than along the steeper, harder north shore, and even here they are usually less dense than they are on earthier shorelines. But where they flourish, a system of life grows up around them that is fairly simple but nonetheless revealing. First, the web of roots helps anchor the shoreline, giving the system's environment some promise of continuity. A film of algae spreads over the leaves of the eelgrass meadow. Bacteria cultures grow on the algae. On this lush pasture feed hordes of zooplankton—microscopic animals larger and more complicated than the algae and bacteria. Meanwhile the larvae of clams and snails attach themselves to the eelgrass leaves. On them and the zooplankton feed various species of shrimp and fish, while some species of waterfowl feed on the leaves themselves.

In the summer of 1931 a change in the salinity and temperature, it is thought, of Alantic coastal water brought on a bloom of microscopic marine fungus. The fungus, a parasite, invaded the eelgrass meadows and devastated them. Nobody, at the time, gave much thought to the consequences for the unseen colonies of algae, bacteria, zooplankton and larvae. But it was widely, and indignantly, reported that the population of Brant geese, an attractive game bird, shrank during the next few years to one-fifth its old, abundant number.

Up the estuary toward Isle d'Orleans and the freshwater reaches of the river, the salt-water eelgrass thins out naturally and finally disappears. Meanwhile other seed or pollen bearing plants have taken over the shallows of the Saint Lawrence. The brackish waters of the upper estuary are a buffer zone. Like the eelgrass, some salt-water varieties of phytoplankton breach the estuary this far but die if they go farther. Some freshwater phytoplankton can tolerate the growing concentration of salt this far down the river, too, but no farther, and like them, a few of the more complicated freshwater plants have adapted to the brackish water of the buffer zone. One of them, Canadian water-thyme, is a fairly close relative of eelgrass with a less active taste for salt. Another, this one a short-stemmed variety of wild rice, has never been found beyond the Saint Lawrence and the streams that run into it. Like the fleabane described in the previous chapter, this strain of wild rice seems to be a true native of the Saint Lawrence Valley.

The wild rice and the fleabane, as it happens, are also a good illustration of the ambiguity on the borderline between the water plants and land plants of the upper river. The fleabane lives on a ledge constantly soaked but never submerged by the tidewater, and is therefore regarded as a land plant. The rice grows mainly under the water, which understandably makes it a water plant. But there are varieties of fleabane that grow half-submerged in marshes. Moreover, fleabane belongs to the family of compound flowers, of which there are a number of maritime varieties. One of these, a small, pale yellow plant called the estuary-beggar-tick, grows in widely scattered clusters from Gaspé to Isle d'Orleans. The rice, of course, belongs to the grass family, and there are scores of grasses that live partly or entirely under the water.

Nearly all the plant families that grow in the Saint Lawrence Valley, in fact, have members living in the river or the marshes that here and there fringe its shores. Some, among them various kinds of pondweed and water plantains, live completely submerged in the water. Others, rushes and flimsier plants like naiads, starwort and wapato, have their roots in the bottom mud and their leaves in the sunlight. A few plants are virtuosos. Bladderwort lives in one form on dry, open ground. In another form it lives underwater, floating without even a root tendril connecting it to the earth. And in a third form it lives rooted on the bottom of the river with its leaves floating on the surface; if the water level falls, it survives in the open, an amphibian.

The amphibian variation of bladderwort also seems to be a predator. Vessels on the undersides of its leaves are so made that moveable lips can open and close around small bladders. When they close, they trap plankton in the bladders. The phytoplankton are far and away the most numerous form of plant life in the upper river, just as they are in the estuary, but the bladderworts are the most ingenious. They close the cycle of plant life in the river, so to speak.

THE LOOK OF THE RIVER

The Saint Lawrence river is a natural highway into the heartland of
the North American continent. Since the days of the earliest explorers
man has sought to improve this highway and to make it more suitable
for travel. Canals around the various rapids were dug in the early
18th century and alterations of the river have been continuous since
that time. With the building of the St. Lawrence Seaway in the 1950's
man has achieved nearly complete control over this once wild river.

Three environments

The Saint Lawrence river has undergone radical alteration at the hands of man. However, even in its natural state it possessed three separate and distinct sections each with its own environment: the high river, the valley, and the estuary. As a river ages it cuts its channel deep and wide as erosion from the moving water cuts away any irregularity in the banks or river bottom. The river also tends to eliminate any bends since the river bank at this point is subject to extensive erosion. The Saint Lawrence is a young river flowing in an old valley and thus has not had time to erode the valley floor.

Here the river crosses the Frontenac Axis near the 1000 Islands flowing rapidly through a valley with many islands and irregularities, see cross-section above.

Near Three Rivers, the St. Lawrence flows over the bed of the old Champlain Sea. The river banks are flat, the channel relatively shallow and the flow is slower than before.

In the estuary the St. Lawrence almost becomes a huge lake. High banks, a slow rate of flow and the tide caused by the influx of sea-water alter the marine environment.

The growth of Montreal

Montreal Island is situated in the middle of a flat plain that extends from the Atlantic to the Great Lakes. Of special importance in the growth of Montreal is the topography of the surrounding land. The underlying rocks date from the Ordovician and comprise various types of limestone. At the end of the Devonian era, volcanic intrusion created what is now Mount Royal. Surrounding this central peak the surface land forms are Pleistocene, sloping from the sides of the mountain to the water level.

◄ *In addition to the routeways offered by the Saint Lawrence and Ottawa rivers and their valleys, reaching west, north and east, the gap between the Adirondacks and New England Mountains, occupied by the Richelieu River and Lake Champlain, give access to Hudson Valley and New York.*

▼ *This map indicates the slope of the land surrounding Montreal. Land with slopes exceeding ten per cent or below one per cent is poor development terrain. Montreal's growth from its riverbank origin has been directly affected by these factors.*

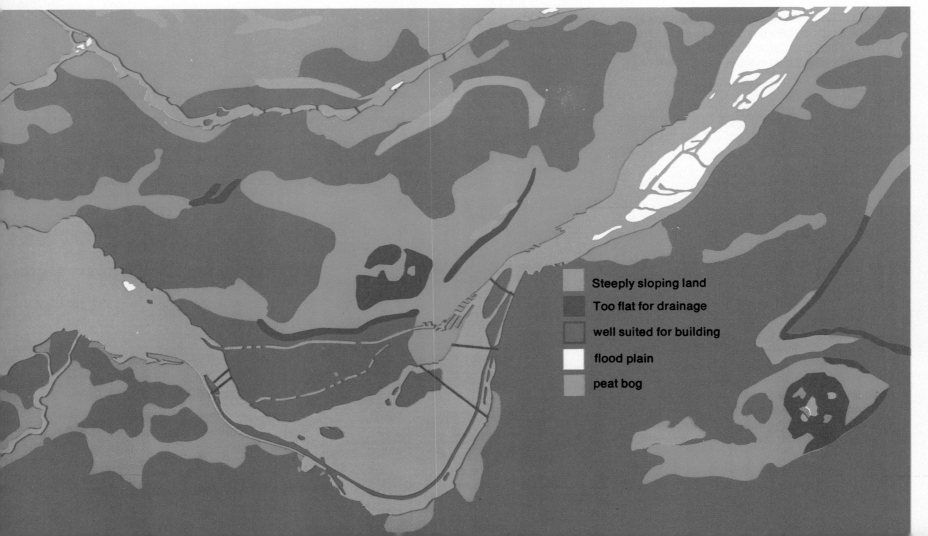

Steeply sloping land

Too flat for drainage

well suited for building

flood plain

peat bog

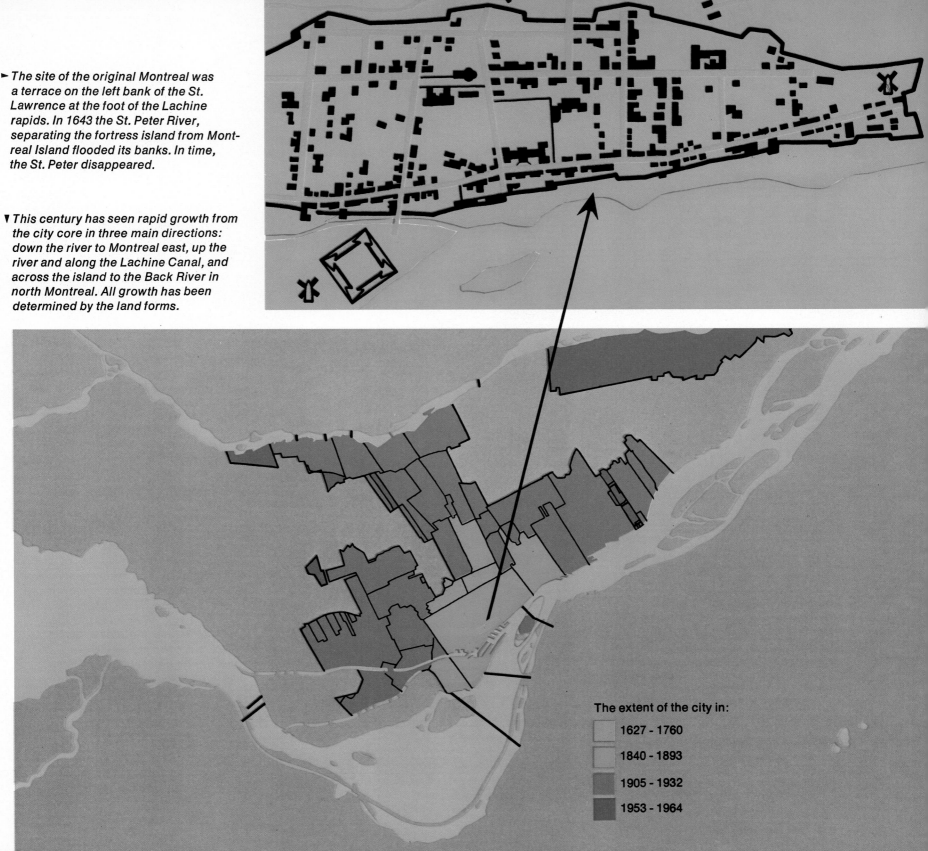

► The site of the original Montreal was a terrace on the left bank of the St. Lawrence at the foot of the Lachine rapids. In 1643 the St. Peter River, separating the fortress island from Montreal Island flooded its banks. In time, the St. Peter disappeared.

▼ This century has seen rapid growth from the city core in three main directions: down the river to Montreal east, up the river and along the Lachine Canal, and across the island to the Back River in north Montreal. All growth has been determined by the land forms.

The extent of the city in:

1627 - 1760

1840 - 1893

1905 - 1932

1953 - 1964

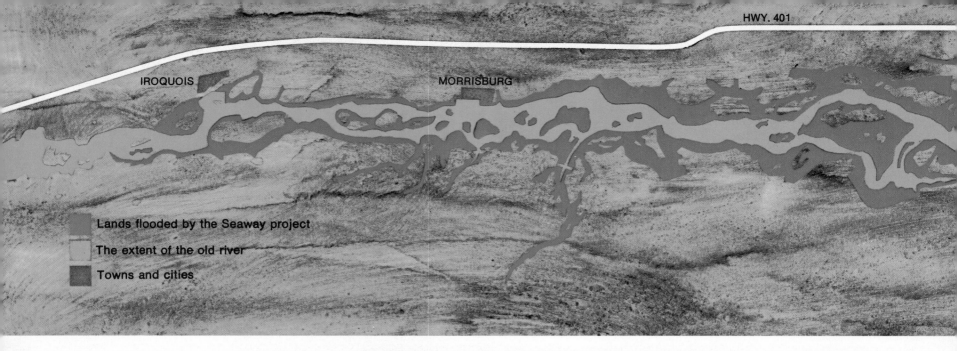

IROQUOIS   MORRISBURG   HWY. 401

Lands flooded by the Seaway project
The extent of the old river
Towns and cities

◄ Before commencing the Seaway project, engineers knew that by filling the power pool between Iroquois and Cornwall, they would submerge nearly 20,000 acres of countryside along the northern shore of the river where some 6,500 people lived. Eventually, agreement was reached on land compensation and all the families were given alternative methods of evacuation; rehabilitation on higher ground, a straight cash settlement, or a combination of the two.

Taming the river

In the Great Lakes–St. Lawrence navigation system, a total descent of 602 feet from the level of Lake Superior to sea level is divided into several parts: drops of 356 feet between the various lakes, a drop of 226 feet from Lake Ontario to Montreal, and a gradual decline of 20 feet between the city of Montreal and the Atlantic Ocean.

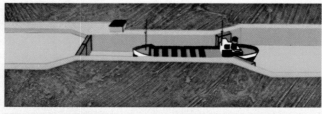

Diagrams on the left indicate how ships enter the lock at low water level, and are imprisoned inside the lock gates; the water escapes from the upper water level until the ship can advance into the upper level lock. Seven new locks were built under the relatively recent Seaway project, affording a total lift of 224 feet. Each lock is 860 feet long, 80 feet wide, and 30 feet deep. The new locks can accommodate cargo vessels carrying up to 25,000 tons.

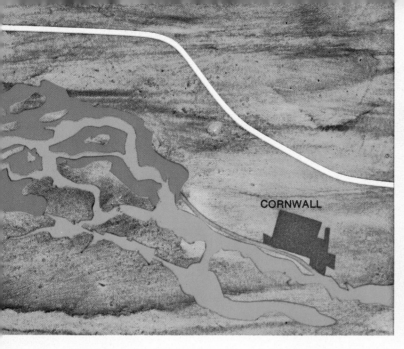

CORNWALL

▲ *The five Great Lakes comprise a huge inland sea with a water surface of 95,000 square miles and a coastline of 8,300 miles, constituting the rich industrial and population centre of North America. The map above indicates the extent of Seaway inundation: the towns of Iroquois and Morrisburg had to be relocated, and new towns such as Ingleside and Long Sault sprang up.*

▶ *Four power dams have now been constructed and are in full operation: at Iroquois, Long Sault, Cornwall and Beauharnois. The Iroquois Control Dam is designed to regulate the flow of water out of Lake Ontario, a control previously exerted by natural rock ledges which have been removed to provide deeper and wider channels for navigation. The Long Sault Spillway Dam combines with the large Moses-Saunders Power Dam at Cornwall to regulate the level of the artificially created Lake St. Lawrence. The Beauharnois Power Dam further downstream helps to control the complex Beauharnois Power Canal and Lock system. At the same time, locks have been built in the Canadian section of the Seaway, aiding deep-bottomed, ocean-going vessels to make the transition from the low-lying Atlantic and coastal stretch of the Saint Lawrence to the high water levels of the Great Lakes.*

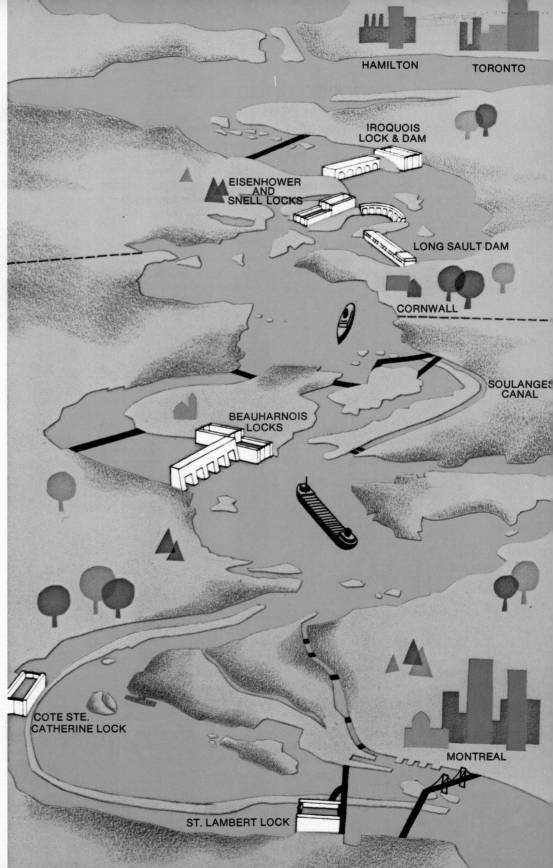

HAMILTON   TORONTO

IROQUOIS
LOCK & DAM

EISENHOWER
AND
SNELL LOCKS

LONG SAULT DAM

CORNWALL

SOULANGES
CANAL

BEAUHARNOIS
LOCKS

COTE STE.
CATHERINE LOCK

MONTREAL

ST. LAMBERT LOCK

The unspoiled environment

The speed with which a river flows along its channel determines the type of life found both in the river itself and along the shore. Before the construction of the seaway the St. Lawrence was a fast-flowing river which contained all the species of plant and animal life adapted to this environment. The damming of the river during seaway construction, however, has resulted in a massive transformation of the river. Now a slow-moving river with many wide marshes along its banks, the whole character of plant and animal life in the valley has changed almost overnight. The full implications of the seaway construction are not yet known, the illustrations at right indicate the extremes of the two possible alternatives.

The effects of pollution

Advocates of the beneficial effects of the seaway construction on the natural environment contend that the large marshes and lakes created by the dams will result in an ideal environment for many birds, plants, shore animals and fish. While the shallow water is able to provide an excellent environment for many species it will only do so as long as man controls his own use and misuse of the river. The ideal situation depicted in the drawing above can easily be turned into the hopeless desolation pictured at right. Pollution and a disregard for the requirements and welfare of the plants and animals which exist in the river could result in the complete destruction of many forms of life found in the St. Lawrence.

The lily-leaf caterpillar is common in quiet water. They make tiny leaf-cases from water lily leaves which serve both as a home and as a source of food for the insect.

Ten-spot dragonflies are found along most rivers and lakes where they feed on small insects. Dragonflies deposit their eggs on the surface leaves and stems of water plants.

One of the larger wheel-snails, three coiled snails live in protected bays, pools, marches, and swamps. These snails lay a hundred or more eggs in a single gelatinous mass.

Stigeoclonium and carteria are two types of algae found in sewage polluted waters. The varieties of algae present depends on the degree and type of water pollution.

During part of their life American eels live on the muddy stream bottom. Carp are also found in muddy water and thought to stir up the bottom to the detriment of other species.

The mudpuppy spends most of its life on the stream bottom feeding on eggs and small insects. The red gills become enlarged to help the mudpuppy breathe in oxygen-poor water.

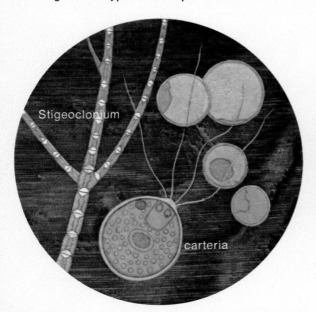

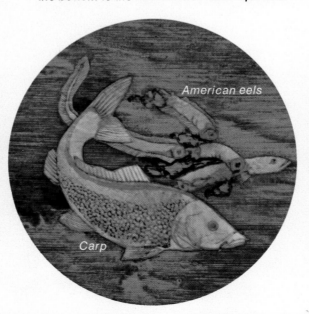

A raccoon digs up turtle eggs buried in the sandy river bank.

PART FOUR / **ANIMAL LIFE**

8 MARINE ANIMAL LIFE

A nylon stocking held open for ten minutes against the tidal stream of the Saint Lawrence estuary will net a fair mixed haul of zooplankton, the animal counterparts of the phytoplankton that dominate plant life in the estuary. The zooplankton, too, are invisible to the unaided eye. But when the toe of the stocking is turned inside-out into a glass of water, the trapped animals will thrash around, and the water will shimmer with motion.

Under a microscope, a drop from the glass will reveal a miniature bestiary. The smallest of these animals are creatures of a single cell, amoeba, the animal equivalent of the simple algae in phytoplankton. They are the least agile of the zooplankton, getting around by waving a false foot that is simply an elongated swelling of the cell wall. Amoeba eat bacteria. So do zooflagellates, slightly more complex single-celled creatures with one or more tails that thrash them through the water. Ciliates, slightly larger and more complex still, have outgrowths thin as hairs around their bodies, and in some cases grow shells. All ciliates eat bacteria, but some ciliates eat other ciliates too. There are more cannibals afloat than ashore.

From time to time, at no set season, these single-celled creatures "bloom" much as phytoplankton do, and then they come to dominate the water, outnumbering all other animals and plants. Usually, though, the most numerous zooplankton are rather more complicated creatures of several cells. Some are rotifers, so called because they beat the water with a double ring of hairs that look, in motion, like revolving wheels. Male rotifers are rare and highly specialized; their bodies amount to little more than a penis and a sperm sac. Rotifers are outnumbered by copepods, miniscule crustaceans that look like angry shrimp. Sometimes copepods make up more than eighty per cent of the zooplankton, and every copepod seems to be perpetually hungry. A hunting copepod sweeps its prey into its mouth with hairy antennae that gather every living particle within range, including its own young. Such larval copepods are called nauplii. They are part of the zooplankton, as are the larvae of several other creatures, including flatworms, polyps, oysters, barnacles and even eels.

Zooplankton are easier to preserve in the laboratory than phytoplankton, one reason why a few of the simplest questions about animal life in the river and the estuary are less controversial than the same questions about plant life. There seems to be no dispute, for instance, about the variety and fertility of zooplankton that have invaded the estuary from the sea. This, marine biologists assume, is the historic route taken by all forms of animal life on the evolutionary trip from the ocean to the land, but a route that very few species are now able to follow.

Changes in the salt content, temperature and chemical behaviour of estuarine water stop many kinds of oceanic zooplankton at the river mouth. But the few varieties that survive in the estuary grow more abundant populations in the same amount of water. Many of these varieties, which include all the forms described above, have evolved into true estuarine species. They can survive, that is, neither upstream in fresh water nor beyond the estuary in undiluted sea water. These highly specialized creatures are thought by some marine biologists to be "conservative" species that migrated from the oceans during the earliest stages of animal evolution. But much of the most recent speculation about the origins of life has been pointing toward the estuary as the likeliest scene for the marriage of molecules that begat the first living substance. The flow of the tides washes a constantly renewed broth of organic mineral compounds across the mud of most estuaries, while from upstream the river brings down landwater charged with silt that settles over the estuarine mud in a fine rain of solid particles. Here, according to the distinguished American biophysicist J. D. Bernal and others, conditions may have been better than anywhere else for the construction of unusually big molecules and their organization into small cells of living matter. This is far from proved; but if the mud of some estuary should turn out to be the place where life began, then the true estuarine zooplankton may be older than the animals of the ocean they are thought to have descended from.

These natives of the estuary differ from their deep sea relatives mainly by their size. In comparison they are very small, almost dwarfs. The same is true of most other animal groups that live only in the estuary. Dense colonies of animals populate the bottom mud, for instance, and the true estuarine species among them are similarly dwarfed. They include many micro-organisms that look like some of the zooplankton, but are adapted to life on the bottom by stalk-like tubes that hold them in place. Zooflagellates and ciliates have made such an adaptation. So have some colourless diatoms, which are closer to animals than plants since they take in—eat, in a sense—the organic substances that keep them alive, rather than manufacturing these substances as plants do. The mud also shelters colourless bacteria, (probably best described as animals for the same reason), that multiply at an incredible rate. A gram of mud scraped from the rich surface film of the mudbed has been reported to contain five billion bacteria cells. Since these bacteria increase between five and six times in twenty-four hours, it seems likely that they would attract neighbours of large appetite, and that is indeed the case.

All these bottom-dwelling creatures feed on each other, and on organic matter dropped from the water above. The zooplankton in estuaries are reported by the few biologists who have observed them to be relatively slow, awkward hunters. They apparently catch and eat little more than half the phytoplankton that blossoms around them. The rest dies, in time, and settles towards the bottom. The mud-dwellers eat some of this decaying vegetable matter, along with the corpses of animals that have died in the water above. Altogether, according to J. W. Kanwisher, of the Narragansett Marine Laboratory, about one tenth of the living matter that grows in the water is eaten by the animals that live in the mud below.

Along with the microfauna, the animals may include a variety of larger, more elaborate creatures. Many are larval stages of animals that normally live in the mud as adults. By some inbuilt regulator they tend to sink as they approach maturity, and then to emerge as fully developed oysters, barnacles, clams, crabs, shrimps, snails and worms. As larvae, they have all foraged for their food; as adults, the shellfish are filter feeders. They suck in a constant stream of water, use the organic matter their digestive systems can filter out, and expel the rest. The shrimps, snails and worms, a little more mobile, tend to be deposit feeders. Like most other animals, they look for concentrations of food. For both types, though, much or in some cases all of their food is in the form of dead and decaying particles raining from above. This constant, heavy rain is called detritus. Some scientists are beginning to suspect that the organic balance of water may depend as much on detritus as it does on living organ-

isms. This seems to be especially true of the estuary, where the rain of detritus falls more heavily than anywhere else. Here, says Rezneat M. Darnell, an American biologist who has made a special study of organic detritus, the water might better be thought of as "a thin mud containing many nutritious opportunities for the consumer species."

Just how the consumer species arrange themselves on the bottom of the Saint Lawrence estuary has yet to be explored. Although the usual ways of conducting this kind of exploration tend to destroy the communities to be studied by dredging them up, some intriguing new ways seem to be at hand. Marine biologists in the United States, for instance, are experimenting with underwater television microscopes.

The pattern of consumer species on the shorelines of the Saint Lawrence, from Anticosti Island to Three Rivers, has been traced by E. L. Bousfield, a Canadian biologist. From the forms of life on the beaches, he feels that the estuary falls naturally into three zones, or regions. The cold salt region, as he describes the seaward zone, reaches from the mouth of the estuary to the vicinity of Baie St. Paul on the north shore, and of Rivière du Loup on the south. Because cold, salty water penetrates much farther up the north shore than the south, the animals that give life in this part of the estuary its special character are the arctic wedge clam, the short-necked clam and the smaller, pure white clam called the chalky macoma, the six-rayed starfish and several species of midget shrimps, among them the opossum shrimp. But the beaches are colonized by other species in only slightly smaller numbers, including larger shrimps, sea urchins, sea cucumbers, crabs, including the hermit crab, and several kinds of marine worms. Near the rivermouth rock barnacles and edible periwinkles grow all the way up the beach to the highwater line. They disappear, though, a short distance up the river, a sign that already the water of the estuary is beginning to change, even though the cold salt zone reaches inland another hundred miles or more.

Still other species that grow abundantly in this zone cross the frontier to grow in almost equal numbers upstream in the next zone, the brackish region. They include creatures that tend to cluster around dense growths of brown seaweed, shellfish such as the common blue mussel, the northern rough periwinkle, the notched acorn barnacle, several kinds of clams, and an associated species of marine worm. The seaweed disappears about half way up this stretch of the estuary, and with it the animals that colonize its neighborhood. Upstream, toward the inland frontier of the brackish region, there are several varieties of midget shrimps and other small crustaceans, all salt-water species, and some small mussels and clams, including the long-necked clam. On the entire shore, only one animal was found in the brackish zone and nowhere else, a midget shrimp called *Mysis stenolepis*—one of the true estuarine animals described earlier. Similarly, only a single animal seems to have penetrated the shoreline from the freshwater reaches of the river, a tough, leathery bug known as the water boatman.

The average salinity of the brackish zone is about twenty parts of salt per thousand, but toward the upper end of this zone dilution by fresh water takes place very rapidly. Beyond the tidal divide near the downstream end of Isle d'Orleans the water has no more than a trace of salt, and the animals of the shore are freshwater species that have adapted to the rise and fall of the tide. The most prominent are freshwater mussels and clams, among them several varieties of finger-nail clams. Small crustaceans abound, including many kinds of miniature shrimps and crayfish. Mayfly and caddisfly nymphs are plentiful, along with the larval and adult stages of many other flies, waterbugs and beetles; so are planarians and leeches. When the first leeches appear along the shore upstream from Quebec City, the last tinge of salt can be assumed to have vanished from the water. Leeches are one of the few forms of aquatic animal life that have left no close relatives in the sea. They have adapted totally to fresh water, and salt kills them quickly.

All the other aquatic animals that make up the drifting zoo-plankton, the burrowing communities in the bottom mud and the mixed colonies along the shore have both salt and fresh water branches in their families. The related species differ very little in looks or habits, but for the fresh water varieties the salt water of the estuary is more than an alien country; it is a death zone, one that only a few can enter, and these not very far. "The majority of animals living in rivers probably do not tolerate variations in salinity greater than one part in ten thousand, and disappear at the head of the estuary," says Melbourne R. Carriker, of the Woods Hole Marine Biological Laboratory, in an extensive survey of estuarine life published in 1967. "A few others," he says,

"survive where the salinity rises to five parts in a thousand; none survives where the salinity goes above nineteen parts in a thousand." In the Saint Lawrence, this is the salt content near the margin between the brackish and salt regions of the estuary.

The reason for the deadly nature of the salt barrier lies in the fundamental balance of the animals' cells. In fresh water, the cells are richer in mineral salts than the water around them. Since the surrounding water tends to pass constantly through the cell walls by osmosis, the animals have had to evolve ways to retain their salts while getting rid of excess water. Otherwise, they would become progressively diluted until they simply washed away.

For sea-water animals, the problem is reversed. In their case the surrounding water tends to be richer in mineral salts than their own cells. Accordingly, they have evolved ways to get rid of excess salts without losing the relatively dilute water of their own cells. Otherwise, they would become progressively clogged with minerals and end by choking on their own juices.

Clearly, then, when an aquatic animal crosses the frontier between salt and fresh water, its own organs set about killing it by working the wrong way. The fatal consequences are so logical and seemingly inevitable that they make the exceptions all the more curious. There are only a few exceptions, none of them, apparently, among the small drifting animals, the shellfish, or the crustaceans. But several free-swimming fishes of the sea are celebrated for seeking out the fresh water streams where they were born before spawning their own young. They are known as the anadromous fishes, and in the Saint Lawrence and its tributaries they include the American shad, the alewife, the tomcod, the smelt, the Atlantic sturgeon, and more notably the Atlantic salmon, the striped bass and the sea lamprey.

All these species, and a few others, are obviously equipped to avoid the usually fatal results of crossing the frontier between salt and fresh water, since they do so compulsively at least twice during their lives, and in some cases more often. How they work this considerable marvel is not yet known, although biologists have long believed that this change, along with several others that prepare the fish for crossing the frontier, is controlled by pituitary hormones, the master hormones secreted by a small gland at the base of the brain. Now confirmation of the role played by hormones may be forthcoming from an unexpected direction. Sea birds can drink salt water, a point that was until recently controversial. They get rid of the excess mineral salts thus trapped in their systems not by some special adaptation of their kidneys, as everything known until now about the organs of higher animals would suggest, but through a pair of simple nasal glands. When the bird has been drinking sea water, the glands drip a highly concentrated solution of salts. When the birds drink fresh water, the glands shrink and stop dripping. Sea birds, that is, have an instantly reversible mechanism for making the switch from salt water to fresh, or from fresh to salt—a switch that quickly kills nearly all water animals except the anadromous fishes. In the case of the birds, there is convincing evidence that the signal to turn the salt glands off or on is given by pituitary hormones. These are the same hormones that appear to be involved in all the changes that prepare the anadromous fishes for their journey across the saline frontier.

Here, it seems, is a likely starting point for a wider understanding of migratory fishes. While it may seem improbable that hitherto unseen glands will be discovered in fishes by tracing the neurochemical route taken by a series of hormones, it seems even less likely that dripping glands could be overlooked for so long in birds. There are easier things to see than drops of salty water dripping from fish. Moreover, the combination of a hormone signal and a simple gland would yield, if it happened to be found, an elegant interpretation of what "locked in" the so-called "landlocked" fish.

The ouananiche, by far the best-known of the few fish native to the Saint Lawrence and its tributaries, is identical to the sea-going Atlantic salmon in every respect but one; the ouananiche never leaves a few streams, chiefly the upper reaches of the Saguenay and Lake Saint John, to make the conventional migration to the Atlantic. So the ouananiche is described as a landlocked fish, along with the varieties of white perch and striped bass that never leave fresh water, and a few others. Yet these fish are no more landlocked than any other fish in the Saint Lawrence, although they may have descended from fish blocked

Marine animals must maintain a balance between the salt in their body and the salt in the water. Fresh water fish have more salt in their body so do not drink water. Salt-water fish have less salt in their system so take in water. The lug worm maintains a natural balance.

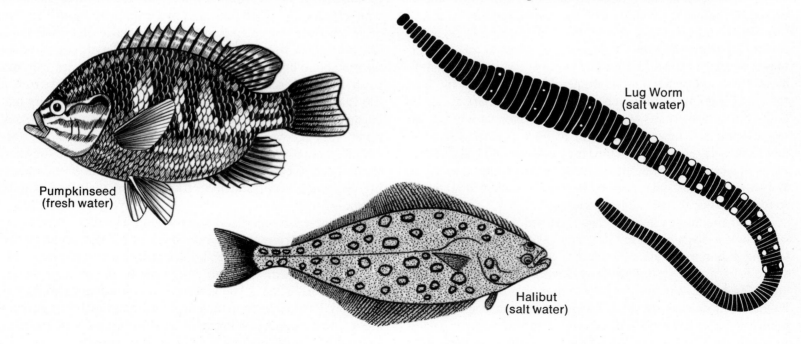

Pumpkinseed
(fresh water)

Halibut
(salt water)

Lug Worm
(salt water)

from the sea by landslides, glacial debris or some other accident in the fairly distant past. Suppose that is what happened. Suppose, too, that those truly landlocked fish were equipped to make the change from salt to fresh water and back again by simple salt glands, triggered by hormones, that shrank when the fish were in fresh water. Such a mechanism, never used, would be more likely to wither away. Now suppose the river opened a new channel to the sea. Without the salt-gland device, the fish would still be as landlocked as they ever were, even with the currents of the Saint Lawrence pushing them relentlessly eastward toward the open sea.

However the ouananiche may have become landlocked, it now belongs to a fairly populous class, the freshwater fish of the Saint Lawrence. Aside from the anadromous fish returning to spawn, the salt water fish that enter the estuary but turn back when they reach the brackish zone come in large numbers but few species: cod, plaice, haddock, hake, herrings, a few kinds of eel, and a handful of others. Atlantic tomcod and killifishes, though not anadromous, seem able to wander freely between the salt and fresh water regions of the river. But the purely freshwater species, none of which ventures far into the brackish waters of the estuary, outnumber the salt water species ten to one. They include many of the more affectionately regarded Canadian gamefish, such "fighting" fish as pickerel, muskellunge, striped bass (a landlocked variety), white bass, smallmouth bass, rock bass, and white perch, a member of the bass family. Sea-going white perch also enter the estuary from the Gulf, but return to salt water. The freshwater variety on the upper Saint Lawrence are thought to have reached the river, and then Lake Ontario, from the Hudson River and Lake Champlain, emerging on the Saint Lawrence near Montreal in 1950. Why a species that enters the estuary made such a long detour to reach the upper river, nobody knows.

But if the Saint Lawrence has recruited one new gamefish, sportsmen suspect the river is losing others. Flabby, bottom-feeding fish are certainly abundant, among them gar, shad, suckers, carp, catfish, bullheads, sticklebacks, sunfish, crappies, and a few more. Whether they are responsible for changing the balance of species in the Saint Lawrence, a change sport fisherman suspect to have taken place only in recent years, is harder to say. Fishery technicians sometimes use a measure they call a single net haul to report the probable frequency of species at a particular point in the water. A single net haul on the Saint Lawrence in 1930 was reported by the State of New York Conservation Authority to be eighteen mooneyes, ten bullheads, two alewives, two northern pike, two suckers and two sunfish.

Certainly the big trout and landlocked salmon that once flourished in the Saint Lawrence have long been extinct or nearly so, and it now seems only a matter of time before the largest animals to penetrate the river are gone as well. Cartier drove his small ships to Stadacona through herds of walrus, seals and white whales that swarmed the water like caribou on the barrenlands. Until this century all three seagoing mammals were still fairly abundant in the estuary, an important source of income for Gaspésian fishermen. They hunt white whales there even now, but sometimes a season goes by without a kill. The white whale, a dolphin species, is also called the beluga, and once it was widely known to mariners by yet another name; the Saint Lawrence whale.

Beluga have been sighted near Montreal, if the few reports are accurate, but their normal range ends around the mouth of the Saguenay. The reason has always seemed obvious, since the wide estuary has more food and more space to hunt it in that narrower river. But there is now some evidence that the beluga, like most other water animals, may actually have been avoiding the metabolic dangers of crossing the frontier between salt and fresh water. A school of porpoises that were moved from a Florida estuary to an inland freshwater pool a few years ago began to blister, and their eyes turned milky. Returned to salt water, they recovered their health quickly. Biologists who examined them found their skin cells pulpy, and assumed they had almost become casualties of their own kidneys —they were retaining too much water and too little salt, and their bodies were beginning to dilute.

But these are superficial observations. The real nature of the beluga, a big terminal link in the mesh of life that animates the Saint Lawrence, is no better known than the real nature of the smallest links near the base of the mesh, the strange, fierce, zooplankton. What is "remarkable" about attempts to understand this basic element in the life of the Saint Lawrence, according to the distinguished French-Canadian limnologist Vianney Legendre, is that "nothing much has been done."

9 ADAPTATION AND SURVIVAL

A few opossums ambled into the struggle for living space along the upper Saint Lawrence during the early 1960's. They seem to be thriving, and this seems odd. If indeed it is the fittest animals that survive and evolve toward "higher" forms of life, then how did an evolutionary dropout like the opossum make it to the twentieth century and the Saint Lawrence Valley?

The opossum has been justly called a living fossil. Skulls of opossums that lived in Canada seventy million years ago indicate that this was essentially the same animal that is now clumsily invading the Thousand Islands region. Meanwhile animals the size of dogs evolved into such higher forms as mammoths, ruled the world for a while, and disappeared. Natural selection led a wide variety of evolving North American marsupials to extinction; one, the opossum, failing to make any evolutionary progress at all, survived.

Adult opossums are about the same size as a house cat in early winter, but they lose about half their flesh by late spring. In the Saint Lawrence Valley, where winter temperatures sometimes drop to twenty or thirty degrees below zero, most small warm-blooded animals hibernate. But opossums, while they appear to have made some of the adaptations necessary for hibernation, do not appear to have made them very well. Many of the live opossums sighted here are missing parts of their tails or ears, which from the condition of the stumps have evidently been frozen off. Presumably these dead and maimed opossums were driven into the cold by acute hunger.

But animals in deep hibernation do not get hungry, at least not in the usual sense. Their normal rhythms slow almost to a stop. Their hearts in some cases beat no more than once a minute. The composition of their blood changes, their digestive tracts stop working. From a layer of special tissue called brown fat they draw down just enough energy, all of it converted into heat, to maintain their body temperatures at a few degrees above

The opossum has recently migrated as far north as the St. Lawrence Valley. The babies cling to the mother's fur for months after birth.

▲ *Beetle larvae live in the ground or in decayed wood and are ferocious feeders. Here, a leaf is slowly being eaten away.*

The insect world

Insects are related to crabs and lobsters, possessing a similar kind of skeleton on the outside of their bodies which comprise three parts: head, thorax and abdomen. The thorax has three parts, each with a pair of attached legs, giving the average insect six legs. Over 900,000 species of insects have been identified, making them the most abundant and potentially most destructive animal force on earth. Only about one per cent of insects are harmful, but these destroy about ten per cent of our crops annually. Insects play an important biological role in the delicate balance of nature.

► *Only wingless female aphids emerge from the eggs in spring, producing generations of females all summer. In the fall, winged females begin a new life cycle, producing both males and females.*

Two adult beetles mate at the centre of a clover plant.

▼ *A syrphid fly alights on a buttercup in search of nectar.*

This chrysomilid beetle gnaws its way through a leaf.

freezing. At this temperature the heart of any animal not in hibernation would long ago have stopped beating altogether, and its nervous tissue would have lost the power to respond to any stimulus at all. The animal would be quite dead.

Clearly, hibernating animals must have some kind of inbuilt regulating system to control these adjustments, including a thermostat of sorts to hold their body temperatures just above the threshold where blood starts turning to ice. A few biologists, among them two who have worked on ground squirrels at the University of Toronto, are now sure they have located this regulating system in the hypothalamus, the area of the brain that is connected by a short stalk to the pituitary gland. The agents that first signal the actual adjustments, including the thermostatic ones, are apparently pituitary hormones.

These are hormones of the same group that appear to control the migratory changes in anadromous fish like salmon, and the salt glands of sea birds and reptiles, all of which were described in the previous chapter. Moreover, among the changes these hormones seem to control in hibernating animals is the capacity of their cells to retain greatly increased amounts of water. Fresh water fish must be able to make the same adjustment before they can survive in the sea.

Biologists have always assumed that some animals hibernate for the same reasons that others migrate, simply to evade seasonal changes in climate and food supply that would otherwise destroy them. Both kinds of behavior are tactical variations on the same strategy. Now it appears that the strategy in both cases is based on the same biochemical network, the intricate, highly sensitive network of signals and responses controlled by the pituitary hormones. Such a network calls for elaborate adaptations. These adaptations have never been more valuable to the animals that have made them successfully than they are in the twentieth century. The global environment has changed radically under the influence of a grossly swollen human population that sterilizes much good ground by building over it, and puts much of the rest under crops that are later taken off completely, leaving little winter forage and almost no cover. Animals unable to migrate or hibernate are hard pressed to survive.

The Saint Lawrence Valley is a more crowded theatre than most for this kind of intense human exploitation, and here, certainly, animals that have adapted to migration or hibernation are prevailing over other species.

But now comes the opossum, an animal that almost hibernates, but not quite, and not very well. Apparently seventy million years have not been long enough for the opossum to make all the intricate but essential adaptations. Like the longnose gar, a primitive freshwater fish adapted to migrate as far as the brackish estuary but not all the way to the salt sea, the opossum can usually hole up safely through a mild Saint Lawrence winter, but is apt to lose its tail or its life in a hard one.

The opossum, moreover, is "excessively voracious, and not less cowardly," according to the great nineteenth-century naturalist John James Audubon. Compared to the wolverine, the opossum is not only cowardly but weak; compared to the mink, sluggish; compared to the marten, stupid. Yet the wolverine is extinct in the Saint Lawrence Valley, the mink and marten nearly so. A hundred years ago Audubon reported that the "range" of the opossum, a southern animal, stopped at the Hudson River. Now, judging by a study made at Cornell University a few years ago, there may well be more than a million opossums north and east of the Hudson in New York State. How many there are in the Saint Lawrence Valley is not yet known.

Unknown, too, are the reasons for the opossum's seemingly absurd inclination to compete for living space on this hostile ground. Several naturalists have suggested that an increase in the yearly mean temperature of two or three degrees since the turn of the century accounts for the opossum's northward migration. But the more reflective Cornell study points out that the coldest days maim or kill, not the monthly averages, and on the coldest days the temperature in the valley still plunges as far below zero as it ever did. The opossum has evidently come north despite the climate.

Why, then, has the opossum come north? And having come, why has a primitive animal not much more than half adapted to survive in temperatures that drop far below zero, an animal relatively sluggish, weak and stupid—why has such an animal flourished where superbly adapted, highly competitive animals have dwindled or disappeared? Nobody really knows, but there are a few facts and some conjecture that probably help account for the opossum's odd prosperity. The opossum is able to eat just about anything, live just about anywhere, and reproduce in almost any season. With these strengths (shared by some other prosperous species, notably rats and men) the opossum's inherent weaknesses may almost be irrelevant in the Saint Lawrence Valley of the later twentieth century.

Although the opossum evolved in the age of the dinosaur and has apparently moved into the Saint Lawrence Valley only recently, there may have been opossums in the valley several times during the interval. This is similarly true of a large species of camel, two kinds of elephants, mastodons, mammoths, and sabre-toothed tigers, all of which were fairly common in the middle latitudes of North America until a few hundred thousand years ago. But if they lived here then, the glaciers destroyed all trace of them. For the species that live here now, the history of animal life in the valley began about ten thousand years ago, when the last ice sheet was in retreat.

The first animals to return were colonizing a naked land on the shores of a receding ocean inlet, the Champlain Sea. Not surprisingly they included several marine mammals; the bones of whales and seals have been found well into the Ottawa section of the valley. Not much later they included men, whose bones have been found in a campsite pitched on the shore of the Champlain Sea. By then several amphibian species had no doubt entered the valley, swampy with the runoff from the melting glaciers to the north; reptiles, insects, and such mammals as beavers, muskrats and otters. As the sea dried completely and the mixed forest took over the valley floor, a more varied population of herbivorous insects, reptiles, birds and mammals moved with the foliage, and with them moved the predators that preyed on them and on each other. From the earliest invasion of the nearly barren land until the pines and maples of the mixed forest took over, the plant and animal life of the valley maintained an absolute but fluid balance, constantly adjusted to the resources of the valley's soil, air, water and climate, readjusted to the changing form of the land as the deepening river channel drained swamps or the decaying plants of one generation enriched the ground for the next. Any change in one element was inexorably compensated for by change in another, as though the entire valley were a single, indescribably complex living organism. A thousand years ago, for instance, the ancestors of the Iroquois migrated from the American southeast, bringing to the valley the first fixed human settlements and the first cultivated plants. Their numbers were few, the clear-

ings they burned off to raise maize or squash were small, but on a modest scale their survival by such means changed the balance of life around them. Lice, bugs, mice, crows and other parasites or scavengers flourished mildly on and around the people; so did the strains of bacteria and algae that multiply in the nitrogen-rich runoff from decaying garbage heaps. With the Iroquois settlements, human pollution made its first subtle contribution to the balance of life in the valley.

But the balance, as always, remained fluid. Like plants, animals flourished or declined by a combination of luck, energy and adaptive drive. Despite range maps, nostalgia and other abstractions, the balance of life nowhere came to rest in a "natural" order. The only natural order was, and is, change, a truism that became more strikingly apparent when change was accelerated by some random event like fire or the intrusion of a potent new migrant. The beaver had been such a migrant, reshaping many of the river margins and minor drainage patterns with his wood and mud technology; the maize-growing Iroquois had been such a migrant; and the European settler was such a migrant on a traumatic scale.

Clearing, digging, seeding, damming, killing, paving, building, and generating organic waste in truly protean varieties and quantities, the European settler accelerated change in the fluid balance of nature to a remarkable though as yet incalculable degree. Momentum alone will probably carry this rate of change forward at a quickening pace. For the moment, though, the natural order of animal life in the Saint Lawrence Valley includes these species:

INVERTEBRATES: Worms, snails and slugs seem to be thriving. Many of them, like some flying insects, are really amphibians at one stage of life, but in the valley there are seventy species of land snails alone. They include a few slugs, or snails without shells. Slugs seem to have a good deal of adaptive ingenuity. For better or worse, as an illustration, they have evolved lungs, perhaps the smallest creature to do so.

Insects appear to be more numerous in the Saint Lawrence Valley than anywhere else in Canada with the possible exception of southern Saskatchewan. Although this may simply reflect the vagaries of reporting, no serious study of insect populations in the valley appears to have been made since the nineteenth

The red eft, spotted salamander and red-backed salamander are amphibians found both on dry land in wooded or forested areas, and in wet marshland along the banks of the St. Lawrence.

century. Many are imported, crop parasites that have increased with cultivation—army worms, tomato hornworms, hessian flies, spring canker worms, codling moths, cutworms of various kinds, European corn borers, pear slugs and so on. June beetles, tent caterpillars, and woodland cockroaches are plentiful, as are European praying mantises. The mantis, a bright green to brown insect that passes through a bizarre larval stage in which it resembles a miniature giraffe, has invaded the valley since 1900 via New York. Insects are often more aggressive migrators than larger animals, and in their larval stages they are, of course, superb hibernators.

AMPHIBIANS AND REPTILES: By converting fast, narrow reaches of water, like the Long Sault Rapids of colourful memory, into artificial lakes lined by marsh or swampy land, such unconventional agents of animal prosperity as the Saint Lawrence Seaway Authority have presumably added to the numbers, if not the variety of amphibian species. Since amphibians tend to take their internal temperatures from the water or air, the long sub-zero winters of the valley are a deadly barrier to some varieties.

Lizards approach the Saint Lawrence but do not, at the moment, come all the way into the valley, apparently because the summers are too short for the young to mature. The spotted turtle, on the other hand, which elsewhere ventures no further north than the lizards, has adapted to life in a single reach of the Saint Lawrence, the broad, shallow, marshy passage downstream from Montreal that is known as Lake Saint Peter. The spotted turtles here are thought to be survivors from a warmer, wetter period that lasted about four thousand years after the ice melted, when amphibians of most varieties flourished in the valley.

Like the spotted turtle, several other species seem to thrive now in the old and new marshes along the river. Other turtles are fairly common, as are many kinds of frogs, toads, salamanders, snakes and mudpuppies. There is a Quebec legend, untrue, that mudpuppies have a poisonous sting. They demonstrate however, an unusual case of arrested development. Whereas nearly all amphibians go through a tadpole stage in which they have fishlike tails and external gills, mudpuppies remain in this stage.

Curiously, these animals seem to find the Saint Lawrence a more formidable barrier to migration than many land species do. The terrestrial box turtle and the aquatic turtle have apparently been unable to cross the river from south to north; nor have the Butler's garter snake, the northern dusky salamander nor the northern purple salamander. The swamp tree frog swarms the marshy stretches of both shores as far as the south bank of the Ottawa. East of the Ottawa, though, the same frog does not appear on the north shore of either river. From the swamp at the foot of the south end of Jacques Cartier Bridge, the chirping of swamp tree frogs carries half way across the bridge on a still night. At the far end of the bridge, on Montreal Island, there are no swamp tree frogs, although there are still a few swamps.

Reptiles that live exclusively on dry land are fairly scarce in the valley. Garter snakes are probably the most numerous, followed by brown snakes. Other snakes are rare, and none are poisonous. A few land-dwelling toads and turtles inhabit waste ground where nothing, as yet, has been built.

BIRDS: By and large, human exploitation of the valley has probably helped more birds than it has harmed, although a few species have been extirpated and for many others seemingly benevolent changes have concealed harsh penalties. Passenger pigeons, the most celebrated victims of overhunting, were long ago killed off entirely. The spruce grouse, one of the more widespread game birds in Canada, was extirpated in the valley partly by hunting and partly by the reduction of the mixed forest to open cropland. Unable to switch from a diet that had leaned heavily on coniferous needles and buds, the spruce grouse died out. In the more typical case of the ruffed grouse, a warier bird, its numbers actually increased despite heavy hunting when the forest was first cleared. It preferred the edges of clearings to the forest floor, and second growth to mature trees. Grain fields and orchards merely added to its food supply, and it prospered until the recent vogue for "clean" farming. Now, with ditches and fence lines cleared, hollows drained, and woodlots often used for pasture, ground cover is very scarce and the ruffed grouse appears to have been driven out of the valley.

Ducks in great numbers frequent the Saint Lawrence by ancient habit; the valley lies on one of the major flyways of the continent. For diving ducks, the forced association with a large human population has probably been discouraging. As bottom feeding fish, particularly carp, have increased in the artificially broadened, calmed, and polluted river, they have gradually displaced the diving ducks' normal food supply. A few diving ducks are still present along the river, notably the ring-necked duck and the common goldeneye, but they are vastly outnumbered by species that feed on the surface. These include the mallard and the black duck, for the moment the most fashionable ducks with the hunters, as well as the strikingly handsome wood duck, two kinds of teal, a few shovelers, and scattered representatives of other species.

Of the marine ducks, salt-water species that seldom penetrate the river above the estuary, the most abundant is the eider duck. It sometimes mingles with the great flock of Atlantic snow geese that assemble by an apparently unanimous habit every spring and fall at Cap Tourmente, just downstream from Isle d'Orleans. Ornithologists believe that the entire species converges on this single reach of marsh and rock to break the annual migration between the high arctic and the coast of South Carolina and Georgia. At either end of the migratory route the birds disperse over wide areas; why they convene at Cap Tourmente midway in the journey is an intriguing but probably unanswerable question.

The true sea birds that often patrol the estuary are probably less affected by human exploitation of the environment than most other animals. Fishing fleets may have diminished their food supply; on the other hand they often feed on the entrails and other leavings that mark the fisherman's passage across the estuary. Great flights of gulls and terns often blanch the water in the wake of the boats. Above them fly cormorants and gannets, and now and then an inblown bird from the far ocean, a petrel, an albatross, a shearwater.

Inland along the riverbanks and through the marshes a profusion of shorebirds seems to be multiplying with the changes in the river: bitterns, gallinules, rails, grebes and coots, plovers, snipes, sandpipers, woodcocks, killdeers and marsh wrens. Protected, now, from sportsmen, great blue herons also seem to be becoming more abundant, fishing the marshes for species anglers have no interest in, flying the treeline with their necks doubled and their heads resting on their shoulders.

The herons nest in high trees along the riverbanks, unafraid of the great horned owls and goshawks that terrify smaller birds.

With the exile or annihilation of nearly all carnivorous mammals of any size, these two big birds are probably the deadliest predators, after man, that still hunt the river. They are usually avoided by several smaller varieties of hawks and owls, and by two larger birds that look even deadlier but are not. Bald eagles are fairly common along the river, especially in the Thousand Islands section and near the Gulf. They are to all appearances royal birds and overwhelming enemies, but they prefer fish to flesh, and prefer scavenging for dead fish to hunting live ones. They seem to turn on other birds only when extreme hunger drives them. Now and then they range the same reach of the river as a pair of ospreys, large hawks that are easy to mistake for eagles. Ospreys usually hunt live prey, but their victims are always fish.

Passerine birds, an enormous family of backyard birds that usually thrive close to people, populate the Saint Lawrence Valley in large numbers and varieties. Cardinals, scarce here earlier in the century, are now fairly common. Bobolinks and mockingbirds, both usually thought of as "southern" species, pass through the valley in growing numbers. Several passerine birds that thrive here are partly dependent on people not only for their food, but for their presence. They have been deliberately imported, for one reason or another. House sparrows seem to be more abundant than any other imported species, and common starlings more controversial. Starlings were first released in Canada near Brockville, on the upper Saint Lawrence. Along with birds released elsewhere, they have spread across most of the country. Ornithologists tend to regard the entire adventure as an unforgivable blunder. Starlings not infrequently take over the nests of redheaded woodpeckers and bluebirds. These birds seem to be in decline, and bird lovers think the starling is the villain.

MAMMALS: A few of the "classic" mammals of the fur-trading era survive in the Saint Lawrence region, chiefly on the unpopulated escarpments at the valley's rim or in the thickest marshes. Naturalists see a beaver, an otter, a mink, or a muskrat now and then along the river. There are a few porcupines, some red foxes and raccoons, a very few grey foxes and even the odd brush wolf toward the rim of the valley. White-tailed deer in small bands sometimes cross the valley floor.

But the characteristic mammals of the valley now are clients of the human population, often imported by them—rats, house mice, small and large brown bats, squirrels, chipmunks. Since there are few predators of any size or range left in the valley, the scavengers flourish. Beyond the built-up areas a fairly sizable community of native rodents still maintains itself in the fields and woodlots. The most numerous are native mice: the deer mouse, white-footed mouse, meadow jumping mouse, woodland jumping mouse, red-backed mouse. A few northern flying squirrels sometimes venture down the escarpment into the woodlots.

Snowshoe hares are fairly common in swampy hollows overgrown by cedar or spruce, and there are some European hares and cottontail rabbits in most unbuilt sections of the lowlands. Shrews are more plentiful, and more interesting. The pygmy shrew, the smallest of several varieties that range over much of the valley, may weigh less than an ounce at maturity. Water shrews, not much heavier, have partly webbed feet fringed by stiff hairs that trap small pockets of air. On a placid surface, a shrew so shod can walk on water for short distances. A larger species, known as the short-tailed shrew, builds elaborate burrows and lives out the winters below the snow.

Shrews are primitive animals, but not as primitive as opossums. Nonetheless, some opossums are doubtlessly eating shrews at this moment in the Saint Lawrence Valley. Opossums will eat anything, living or dead. One study of the stomach contents of sixteen opossums found insects, worms, fruit, berries, grass, seeds, green leaves, mammals, trash, acorns, crayfish, snails, birds and some unidentified matter. The naturalist who conducted the study concluded that food supply could not influence the abundance of the opossum, since there was nothing the opossum could not or would not eat. Audubon once bought two dozen opossums to ship to a friend in England, but found before the crate left the country that the older males had gnawed the heads off the younger ones. This strategic ability to take its food where it finds it, along with a willingness to live anywhere from a swamp to an exposed ledge of dry rock, may in time well make the sluggish opossum the inheritor of the domain of nearly all the wild animals that have lived in the Saint Lawrence Valley.

CAMOUFLAGE
AND CONTROL

Scales cover the wings of all *lepidoptera* in overlapping rows,
each scale has a minute stalk which fits into a corresponding
socket in the wing membrane. Moth scales are variable and
sometimes adapted into scent scales. Note the standard structure
and shape of the scales in the detailed photograph above.

NATURE'S TWINS

The viceroy — The monarch

Protective colouration is a common method of survival in nature. The two butterflies on this page look so much alike that birds, their natural enemies, apparently cannot distinguish between the species. The viceroy is smaller, has an additional band on its hindwings, lacks the male monarch's scent glands, and possesses one row less of white spots on the border of its wings. The viceroy's flight pattern is unlike that of the monarch, being a faster-beating flapping, alternating with glides in which the wings are held horizontally and not slanted upward as on the monarch. The viceroy (1) is a popular butterfly frequently seen over open fields from Canada down to the Mexican Gulf during the months of August and September. The viceroy's eggs are deep green, globular in shape and pitted, and are laid individually on the upper or under-leaf surfaces of food plants, usually at the tip of the leaf. These eggs hatch within four to eight days into a larva or caterpillar (2) which resembles bird-dropping—irregular, warty, over an inch long, with a pair of long clubbed, prickled tubercles near the front, black in colour. The larva hibernates for winter and grows through moulting. The pupa stage of the viceroy (3) lasts about two weeks depending upon the temperature and humidity of the surrounding climate. The final metamorphosis—the emergence of the butterfly (4) takes only a few minutes. The butterfly appears with limp moist wings which gradually expand as fluids are pumped through the veins (5).

124

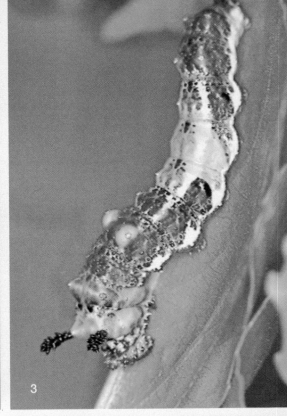

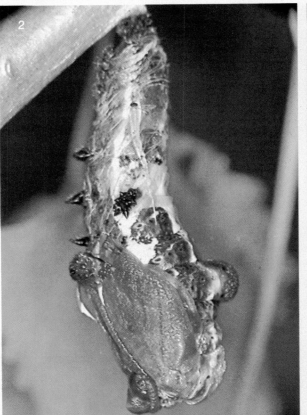

The migrating monarch

The monarch butterfly has long been thought to be inedible by birds because they find the taste offensive. This theory is the subject of continuing research and debate but the remarkable resemblance between these two butterflies has led scientists to assume that the viceroy is also avoided by birds which mistake it for an inedible monarch. The monarch itself is remarkable in that each year it produces up to four generations, the last of which migrates between Canada and the Gulf of Mexico or California. The male produces a mating smell to attract the female by rubbing a small hair on the small scent scales found on each wing.

5
6

Biological control—
Green Lacewings

The green lacewings are a group of mainly medium sized green insects, (one group is, however, brown) with compound eyes. All lacewings are carnivorous and if the eggs were not laid on individual stalks the first born would immediately devour the others. These insects perform an important role in the biological control of aphids. Since the larvae feed primarily on aphids they are called aphis lions. Each larva possesses sharp, pointed mandibles which are grooved along the inner surface so that they form closed tubes through which it sucks its victim's body fluids.

The adult lacewing, grown to its full 0.6", as it appears after mating.

The vital organs of moth larvae are not attacked until parasite reaches maturity.

Moth Larvae

Parasites provide effective control of the number of moth larvae that reach maturity. The parasites enter the larvae and continue to eat the living organism, sparing only the vital organs, until the parasites are ready to assume the pupa stage. They then emerge from the moth larvae and attach themselves to leaves for the next stage of their growth pattern. The moth larva dies shortly afterwards, having never fully developed into a mature moth.

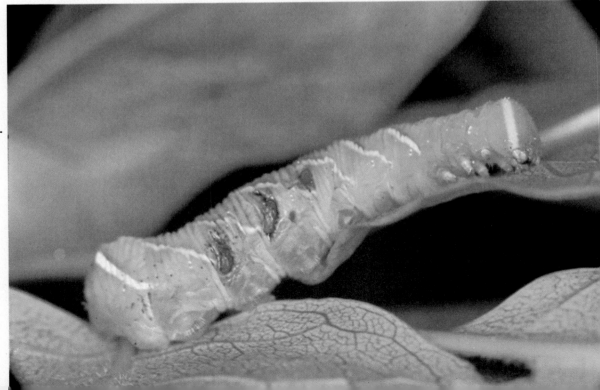

126

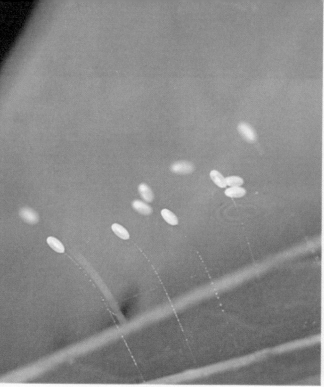

Eggs are placed on silk stalks for safety.

Larvae hatch on the underside of a leaf.

Aphis lions wear their victims' bodies.

Here the larvae of the parasites emerge from the moth larva.

Larvae commence the pupa stage; note skin of dead moth larva.

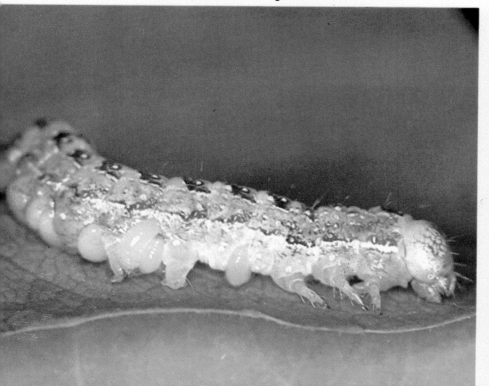

*A tiny mite parasite is feeding
on the body fluids of a living aphid.*

PART FIVE / CONSERVATION

10 WHERE THE RIVER ENDS

The poetic nature of rivers is to endure. They flow like time, one stream recalling the other. "Riverrun, past Eve and Adam's, from swerve of shore to bend of bay," said James Joyce in the opening line of Finnegan's Wake, looking for a symbol to outreach the entire course of life on earth. Since the sixteenth century, writers describing the Saint Lawrence have usually spoken at least once in every book about "the ageless river." A wordless man overlooking a great river tends to feel the same way.

These are the rivers of sentiment. The real nature of rivers is to come and go, sometimes quickly. The Saint Lawrence is probably less than nine thousand years old. Lately come, the river could soon be gone, destroyed by a return of the ice sheet, by uplift in the earth's crust, by a cataclysmic earthquake. Should the river escape a violent end, it will end by choking itself on its own debris.

For the first twenty or thirty years of its life, the young, fast, rock-ribbed Saint Lawrence aged less quickly than most rivers. The soft sediments of the deep submarine channel are nowhere more than seventy-two feet deep, evidence of an unusually slow rate of erosion since the ice age. But in this century the river is aging at a grossly accelerated pace, a result of the forced intimacy between the river and the swelling human population of the valley. General observations about nature should be suspect, but it seems true that everything we do to the Saint Lawrence degrades it.

Nor could anything be more normal. All plants and animals, including man, survive by exploiting their environment and each other. But we are the only population that sets out to pursue survival by understanding rather than instinct. For this tricky enterprise we need knowledge and clarity, and seem to have neither. A few scientists are trying to tell us this. "There is," says Melbourne R. Carriker, of the Woods Hole Marine Laboratory, "an urgency to study estuaries before unenlightened defacement obliterates them, and before it becomes expedient to investigate them primarily as outdoor pollution laboratories."

We have trouble understanding this kind of talk. I have in mind here no superficial irony, but what seems to me a genuine disability to speak or think of "nature" in any but sentimental and poetic terms. How, for instance, are we to consider the results of deliberately aging an ageless river?

Not that anybody knows precisely what the results are; that is just the trouble. But speaking the language of sentiment, loving nature, we are hardly aware that there is any reason to be curious about the actual results so long as the apparent results appeal to our strongest sentiments—so long, that is, as they are pretty or profitable to operate. The short history of the power dams on the upper Saint Lawrence demonstrates this one-dimensional habit of mind fairly clearly.

The progression from a high, hard bank to an eroded and silted shallow, to a marsh, to a swampy hollow, to firm ground where the water formerly ran, is equivalent in a river to the hardening and thickening of the blood vessels that ages an animal. The power dams that now blockade the Saint Lawrence above Cornwall changed the strongest, "youngest" reach of the river into a sluggish lake thirty miles long, the new Lake Saint Lawrence. "The old Saint Lawrence had steep banks and a fast current and good marshes were few and far between," a communiqué from the Ontario government reminded the public at the time, with some pride and complete accuracy. The new lake has a weak current and about forty thousand acres of shallows and marshes.

So aged, this section of the river will probably grow rich in new life. Water plants, fishes and birds are expected to multiply prodigiously. This usually happens in the waters of aging rivers, and there seems to be no reason why it should not happen here. Conservation officials of both Ontario and New York said before the new marshes were flooded that they anticipated such a flowering. The catch of bass, the bag of black ducks, the intense pleasure thousands of visitors take in simply looking on at the wildlife now to be seen here, all tend to confirm the judgments made in advance.

Ontario conservation officials now speak of "a recreational and sporting paradise" where once the barren rapids ran. This is hardly saying too much; almost everybody is delighted. Nobody, on the other hand, seems to be trying to find out what is happening in and to the river. The New York Conservation

Department has "no studies related to specific changes in fish and wildlife resources" caused by the power project; nor has the Ontario Conservation Department; nor, apparently, has anybody else.

For a measure of change that might add to our understanding of the river, studies of fish and birds are a preliminary to discovering changes in the patterns and rates of silting, of biological activity, and of such chemical processes as oxygenation. In the drowned rapids, water from the Great Lakes was tumbled and foamed through the air, a theatrical passage that had the practical effect of charging the water with a fresh supply of oxygen.

Starved of oxygen, water supports a dwindling variety of life, mainly bacteria and other single-celled organisms. Such water is often said to be dead; much of Lake Erie and parts of the other Great Lakes are at this stage, and some of their water reaches the Saint Lawrence. The rapids that once recharged this moribund water are gone. We have replaced them with miles of marsh, incredibly rich, as we have been assured, in new life. The competition for oxygen here, a factor known as biological oxygen demand, or BOD, will now presumably be greater than it is in Lake Erie. Rather than coming back to life, the water from Lake Erie passing through the river may now continue to lose oxygen and die a little more.

In that case, the balance of life in the Saint Lawrence downstream will be seriously deranged by the new paradise upstream. How seriously nobody can say, but the range of possibilities includes the decline of the larger fishes and other underwater animals, the proliferation of microbes and plankton, and the eventual reduction of the river to a long streak of moveable slime. Has this started to happen already? Probably, but at an initial level so low that it would be hard to measure. At this stage, the process is invisible without highly developed knowledge and specialized techniques. The techniques are known, but not used; the process is probably manageable, but we are not trying to manage it.

There is, as it happens, a curious byproduct of this development that is easy enough to see, should anybody care to look. It concerns eels.

Eels are among the few Saint Lawrence fishes that reverse the familiar spawning migration of the salmon and most other anadromous species—the eels live in the river and return to the mid-atlantic to spawn. The mature eels set out for the spawning grounds in high summer. By mid-August eels that live in the upper Saint Lawrence and Lake Ontario are arriving in great numbers at the power dams that barricade the river above Cornwall. To get past the dams the eels have only one way to go; down the concrete tunnels leading to the turbines that turn the dynamos. Driven by the downstream instinct that dominates this phase of their lives, the eels follow the moving water into the turbines. The blades chop them into small pieces, and the mince is disgorged below the dams along with the spent water, now pink and slightly frothy.

There has been one public reference, so far as I know, to the decimation of the upper Saint Lawrence eel population. Decimation, in this case, is an accurate description. The adult eels live in fresh water for eight to twelve years before they set out to spawn. The turbines, accordingly, would seem to be destroying about a tenth of the upper Saint Lawrence and Lake Ontario eel population every year.

Nothing has been heard about them before or since from any of the people who follow the destiny of a few whooping cranes from egg to moult, and who are shocked by the death of a salmon butting its head against a power dam a continent away on the Pacific Coast. The luck of the eel is to look something like a thick water snake or a gorged lamprey, so that while it is in many ways a valuable fish, nobody has ever called it a noble one.

A naturalist who lives part of the year on an island in the Saint Lawrence has told me that the eels are paying the price of progress. This popular idea seems to be hard core of the poetic attitude to nature. It makes a certain amount of sense to base an attitude on sights and smells: killing eels, which are ugly, is natural; letting their corpses drift into Cornwall Bay, where they will offend people, is unnatural. But to conclude that the eels are thereby paying the price of progress is pure nineteenth-century romance. In the present state of the arts that bear on the balance of life, the degradation of the river is an incalculable event. The power dams may turn out to be worth the unknown price they will extract from the river, including the death of the eels, but choosing to call the entire blind adventure "progress" is almost deliberately to discard sense in favour of stirring the verbal mud around.

The Long Sault Spillway Dam is characterized by its distinctive crescent shape.

An engineer controls lock operations at the Long Sault.

◄ *Long Sault Dam controls the water flow to the International Power Dam.*

The St. Lawrence seaway – man alters the face of the river

The Long Sault Spillway Dam, a crescent-shaped concrete gravity dam, is 2,960 feet long and 132 feet high, and barricades the southern channel between Barnhart Island and the American north shoreline. The Dam is located three miles upstream from the Moses-Saunders Power Dam, and combines with the latter to control the level of Lake St. Lawrence. Long Sault Spillway Dam has 32 gates, each having dimensions 52 feet wide and 30 feet high, that can be raised in periods of high water to release the water which is not required for the production of power. The Long Sault Canal, adjacent to the dam, permits deep-draft ocean-going vessels to avoid the dangerous currents and rapids and continue on their inland journey to the lakes. Both the construction and operation of the dam and canal have led to the sprouting of the thriving town of Long Sault along the Canadian north shore.

◄*The Long Sault Canal allows deep-hulled vessels to traverse the inland waterways.*

133

11 MAN AND THE RIVER

Snails of a genus called *Hydrobia*, snug in the mud near the mouth of the Saint Lawrence, feed on rotting bits of dead plants and animals. They suck up everything that comes their way, digest what they need and, like all animals, evacuate the rest. They seem to need nitrogen compounds—proteins—since they digest nearly all the proteins they eat. Carbohydrates, on the other hand, they are evidently unable to use, so they evacuate them.

Nothing is more useful to some kinds of bacteria than carbohydrates, which they need for fuel in manufacturing protein from the nitrogen dissolved in the water. Great numbers of these bacteria colonize the carbohydrates evacuated by *Hydrobia*, where they start manufacturing protein. They are still at it, in many cases, when *Hydrobia* sucks them up along with its own excrement. *Hydrobia* digests the bacteria, rich in protein, and again evacuates the carbohydrates. More bacteria colonize the fresh excrement and start manufacturing protein. *Hydrobia*

sucks them up. . . .

Meanwhile, upstream from the tidal flats, several million less specialized animals do much the same thing. They are the human population of the valley, and their way of dealing with their own wastes runs a similarly circular course. First they flush raw excrement into the Saint Lawrence water system. Then they suck water up from the same system in pipes, consume it, and flush fresh excrement back into the system. They imitate the snails, that is, with one or two strategic contrasts.

Our excrement, unlike the snail's, has been greatly diluted before we consume it. This is just as well, since again unlike the snail we are ill adapted to consume our own excrement. With sufficient dilution it seems to do us little harm, although not even politicians argue that it does us any good.

Perhaps this will not always be the case. There is a hint of perpetual motion about *Hydrobia's* circular eating habit that fascinates technologists looking ahead to such visionary enterprises as interplanetary flight and undersea habitation. A few of them are now casting around for ways to help astronauts and aquanauts do by craft what *Hydrobia* does naturally. But that prospect lies happily with the future. For the moment, *Hydrobia*

For centuries the Long Sault Rapids provided a magnificent display of nature's power – however they made it impossible to sail on the river.

is the only animal definitely known to get much of its nourishment from food it has eaten before, although marine biologists now suspect this talent may be shared by some other snails, worms, and mud-dwelling creatures.

Hydrobia's enviable ability to dine well on its own breakfast is based on a second adaptation. Were the snails to void their wastes in a loose state, as people do, the protein-building bacteria would have to colonize thousands of smaller cellulose fragments suspended in the water, and the snails would be unlikely ever to suck up enough of them to provide a useful meal. But the snails deal otherwise with this valuable material. As the waste from their digestive tracts moves through their intestines, mucus binds it together in short rods. When the rods are voided, a final coat of mucus cements their outside surfaces. Students of the subject call these rods faecal pellets, and they have all the virtues of nationally advertised products, in this case authentically. They are firm, compact, often ornately sculptured by the grooves and ridges of the intestine wall, and, once excreted into the river, all but permanent.

Faecal pellets, thus finely wrought, often last more than a hundred years. Where the underwater population is dense, the mud may contain more faecal pellets than any other material, since *Hydrobia* is not the only animal to have worked out this way of voiding its wastes. Most of the small creatures that live in the underwater mud evacuate their wastes in this form.

As well as snails and worms, they include the vastly more abundant family of filter feeders, animals that run a constant stream of water through their bodies, filtering out such particles of useable food as come their way. If they were to discharge their wastes in a loose state, "it is certain that estuaries would be considerably more turbid than they are," according to the marine biologist Melville R. Carriker. Moreover, filter feeders might recycle faecal particles ad infinitum, slowly starving to death in a futile attempt to emulate *Hydrobia* by endless eating the small meal.

The comparison between filter feeders and *Hydrobia,* on one hand, and us, on the other, can be summed up like this: (1) Among the mud-dwelling population of the Saint Lawrence, some animals are able to eat their own faeces with profit, while the ones that cannot eat them avoid them. (2) Among the human population, nobody has yet taken the trouble to acquire one ability or the other. We eat a small quantity of our own

During the building of the seaway a temporary dam exposed the bottom of the river – the rapids were later destroyed by the seaway.

faeces diluted with large amounts of water, and leave the river to deal with the rest.

This seems, no doubt, a tasteless way to speak, an unsettling sentiment. So it is, in a mild way, and since it is also such a plain observation of fact it may help establish the altogether confusing role of sentiment in any attempt to understand our relationship with the river. Enormous quantities of faecal debris much amplified by other kinds of organic and chemical waste are our principal contribution to the state of the Saint Lawrence. We speak of this as the price of progress and seldom speak or think of it again, unless we are reminded by a bad smell or an ugly sight.

Both, for the time being, are fairly rare. Luckily, because nobody could have foreseen the astonishing capacity the Saint Lawrence has demonstrated for absorbing sewage without letting it show. There are well over two thousand municipalities in the valley, but only a handful of small towns treat their sewage before they flush it into the Saint Lawrence drainage system. Neither Quebec City nor Three Rivers has a sewage treatment plant of any kind. Nearly all the faeces and other decaying by-products of two million Montrealers drift downstream raw.

Applying a standard adopted by the International Joint Commission, the body that regulates waters shared by Canada and the United States, the flow of the Saint Lawrence at Montreal is adequate to handle the raw sewage of fifty-four thousand people. Twenty years ago, when the population of Montreal was hardly more than a million, a provincial ordinance imposed a "formal obligation" on the city to treat its sewage before flushing it into the Saint Lawrence. Quick to comply, the city announced that it had acquired a tract of land for a "major project" that would soon look after the matter. When I inquired after the status of the formal obligation early in 1968, the Quebec Water Board said that while Montreal was treating none of its sewage at that moment, and never had, the Board was "none the less pleased to say that Montreal has recently revealed a major treatment project. . . ."

Looking toward the harbour at Quebec City the degree to which we are polluting our natural environment becomes apparent.

136

Inquiries about the quality of the water, thus enriched, tend to be met by similar replies. Officials in the relevant government departments of Quebec, Ontario and Canada say that no information whatever will be available about water quality in the Saint Lawrence until a study by the International Joint Commission is published.

This disclaimer is not strictly true; an industrial engineer in Montreal, for instance, has for several years been making some analyses of Saint Lawrence water for large corporations and for government bodies. No doubt other experts have been doing the same thing. But it is true that such information, for what it may be worth, is not available to the public. Canadian officials are in the habit of treating their files as their own property when this suits their convenience, as it often does. Since we have no public information act to compel disclosure, unlike the United States, there is nothing much we can do about it. To be fair, we seldom ask questions, and this doubtless seems to the officials concerned to justify their habit of concealing information from us.

In New York State, where disclosure is required by law, some information is available. A report on the international section of the Saint Lawrence and its tributaries includes this description of the Raquette River, which runs into the Saint Lawrence near Massena: "There are periods of up to fourteen hours when the flow in the river . . . is completely cut off. The entire flow during these periods consists of municipal and industrial waste effluents." Among many similar observations, the report describes the "degradation in quality" of the Saint Lawrence at Massena, where "poorly treated wastes from the General Motors-Chevrolet Division aluminum casting plant and the Reynolds Aluminum plant cause a milky, oily appearance to the waters on occasion."

The names here are interesting partly by contrast—in official Canadian usage, industrial plants that degrade the water system do not have names. The Ontario Water Resources Commission says that the information it has about industrial wastes was obtained in confidence from the companies involved. In the unlikely event that this is true, it proposes a novel way to regulate a public resource—by secret agreement with the people who are degrading it. More probably the OWRC has made at least some analyses of its own, but prefers to keep these results secret

too. The premier of Ontario told me in 1967 that until then it had been a fairly common practice of governments to look the other way when large corporations (with large tax bills) broke such regulations as there were to protect the water supply. It had been, he implied, the price of progress.

The Quebec Water Board, which has made no studies of water quality in the Saint Lawrence, does speak of visible, malodorous additions to the water—floating sewage, oil and gasoline slicks, foams of detergent, fibrous masses discharged by paper mills, fertilizers and insecticides. The price of progress on this scale, the Board says, has been pollution of the Saint Lawrence around Montreal that makes the river "unfit for consumption and recreation." Great blooms of algae have in recent years blocked the pipes and filters of Montreal's water works from time to time. Fish strangled in the oxygen-starved waters of the Ottawa float belly-up to the surface every spring. These unsightly events often lead to complaints, like the Board's, about pollution.

But here, it seems to me, we are on a treadmill. What is pollution? Bad sights and smells, mainly, or so it appears from all published reports on the subject. But these are merely symptoms, insults to our sentimental view of the river. What is happening in the water? We don't know. Elsewhere a few scientists may be starting to find out. Speaking of estuaries, the most thoroughly scoured of all river regions, Paul De Falco, Jr., an American microbiologist concerned with public health problems, has said that "what was once a bottomless pit, able to receive all that man could imagine, has now become, in many areas, a septic cauldron of man's wastes."

The Saint Lawrence has not become such a cauldron, either in the estuary or the more vulnerable upper river. Not yet. The most remarkable part of the New York State report on water quality in the Saint Lawrence is the conclusion. Despite its detailed account of wastes added to the river in breathtaking variety and abundance, the report concludes that "gradual increases in chlorides and total dissolved solids have occurred. But otherwise there is no definable change indicating a deterioration or improvement in the quality of the Saint Lawrence River."

While this is clearly not the case downstream, particularly between Montreal and Quebec, even here the river manages somehow to keep itself fairly clean while swallowing protean amounts of sewage. At what real "price" to the balance of the river, we have no idea. Nor, unless we find a way to separate sentiment from our attempts to understand this living balance, will we have any better idea on the day the balance shifts against us.

For now, we watch the Saint Lawrence without seeing it. Defending the poetic virtues of the ageless river, we set afoot conservation schemes that work toward climaxes blinder than myth. In 1900 the population of snow geese arriving at Cap Tourmente each spring and fall was between two and three thousand birds. By then the feeding grounds where the geese congregate were in the hands of a hunting club, *Club de Chasse de Cap Tourmente*. From motives both sporting and altruistic, the members imposed severe curbs on hunting and any other interference with the geese. The region became a private sanctuary where the geese were safe from slaughter by anybody but club members, who limited themselves to small numbers of birds. The Royal Canadian Mounted Police was enlisted to enforce the rules.

The geese multiplied, generation by generation. Pale hosts now sweep down eighty thousand strong on the clay flats between Cap Tourmente and Isle d'Orleans. They spend several weeks pillaging the bullrush stands that grow in stunted forests along the inshore shallows. By the time the geese leave every appearance of vegetation has been stripped from the north shore, not only on the surface but several inches into the mud, where the birds have burrowed for tender roots. During the winter, ice scrapes bare a deeper layer of roots, and in the spring the geese return to dig for these.

The geese and the bullrushes are maintaining a very delicate balance indeed. For the moment, the bullrushes still recover enough growth each summer to feed the geese each fall. But the geese, which once numbered less than three thousand altogether, now return from the breeding grounds in flocks five thousand birds larger than the season before.

Years ago, on their wintering grounds off the Carolinas, when the snow geese were half as numerous as they are now, they fell on several small islands, where they reduced grassy meadows to "shallow, foul pools, completely devoid of vegetation," according to a naturalist who observed their assault. "How many years must elapse before these bare flats will again be clothed with sufficient vegetation to be used as feeding grounds depends upon a number of factors—the soil, wind erosion and water action," he said. "Some of these barrens are known to be four or five years old and yet show little or no sign of vegetation."

Snow geese are noble birds, swift and dazzling in flight though gluttonous aground. When the bullrushes are all gone at last, some of the geese will die in the brown pools where the rush meadows grew, and some will wheel away, violet from below and lovely in all lights, leaving the ageless, aging Saint Lawrence to such natural survivors as *Hydrobia*, the snail, and man, the poet and planner.

Some fifty thousand greater snow geese stop at Saint-Joachim each year – doing immense damage to the plant cover in the area.

GEOLOGIC TIME SCALE

TIME	ERA	PERIOD	EPOCH	THE ASCENT OF LIFE:
	CENOZOIC	QUATERNARY	PLEISTOCENE	
			PLIOCENE	
		TERTIARY	MIOCENE	
			OLIGOCENE	
50			EOCENE	
			PALEOCENE	
100	MESOZOIC	CRETACEOUS	UPPER	
			LOWER	
150		JURASSIC	UPPER / MIDDLE / LOWER	
200		TRIASSIC	UPPER / MIDDLE / LOWER	
250	PALAEOZOIC	PERMIAN	UPPER / MIDDLE / LOWER	
300		PENNSYLVANIAN		
		MISSISSIPPIAN		
350		DEVONIAN	UPPER / MIDDLE / LOWER	
400		SILURIAN		
450		ORDOVICIAN	UPPER / MIDDLE / LOWER	
500				
550		CAMBRIAN	UPPER / MIDDLE / LOWER	

MILLIONS OF YEARS

THE ASCENT OF LIFE: 1, *protozoan*; 2, *jellyfish*; 3, *crinoid*; 4, *cephalopod*; 5, *climatius*; 6, *shark*; 7, *brachiopod*;
8, *seed fern*; 9, *dimetrodon*; 10, *brontosaurus*; 11, *plesiosaur*; 12, *tyrannosaurus*; 13, *taeniolabis*; 14, *diatryma*;
15, *hyracotherium*; 16, *brontotherium*; 17, *oxydactylus*; 18, *pliohippus*; 19, *mastodon*; 20, *man*.

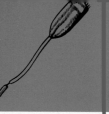

SHORT LIST OF ROCKS, PLANTS AND ANIMALS

The lists on the following pages have been compiled as a basic guide for amateur naturalists intending to explore the wealth of the natural history of the St. Lawrence Valley region. These selected summaries cannot possibly cover all species — there are many thousands of insects alone — but an attempt has been made to include the common life forms and the natural phenomena peculiar to this region. Readers should find it useful to study the lists touching on their sphere of interest, checking off items they have observed during field trips. Those wishing to extend their search will find an extensive Bibliography on pages 153-5, the references listed there contain more detailed information on many specific subjects.

ROCKS

CENOZOIC ERA
Glacial Deposits
Marine Clays
Lake Clays
Till

CRETACEOUS
Rocks found in
the Monteregian Hills
  Peridotite
  Alnoite
  Ajolite
  Okaite
  Carbonatite
  Nepheline Syenite
  Pulaskite
  Nordmarkite
  Magnetite
  Syenite Porphyry
  Essexite
  Gabbro

DEVONIAN PERIOD
Shale

Sandstone
Limestone
SILURIAN PERIOD
Dolomite
Limestone
Shale
Sandstone
ORDOVICIAN PERIOD
Limestone
Shale
Sandstone
CAMBRIAN PERIOD
Sandstone

PRECAMBRIAN ERA
Igneous rocks
Metamorphic rocks

MINERALS
The minerals listed are those most likely to be found in the following regions.

EASTERN QUEBEC
Gold
Pyrite

Asbestos
Limestone
Magnesitic
Dolomite
Brucite
Silver
Copper
Peat
Zinc
Silica
Lead

MONT ST. HILAIRE, QUEBEC
Acmite
Actinolite
Aegirine
Albite
Almandine
Analcite
Ancylite
Andradite
Ankerite
Apophyllite
Arsenopyrite
Astrophyllite
Augite

Barite
Bastnasite
Biotite
Birnessite
Brookite
Burbankite

Calcite
Cancrinite
Catapleiite
Chalcopyrite
Crocidolite

Datolite
Dawsonite
Diopisde
Dolomite

Elpidite
Epididymite
Eudialite

Fluorite

Galena
Genthelvite
Goethite
Gotzenite

Grossularite
Grunerite
Gypsum

Hackmanite
Helvite
Hematite
Hornblende

Idocrase
Ilmenite

Karpinskyite

Lavenite
Leifite
Leucophanite
Leucosphenite

Magnetite
Mangan-neptunite
Marcasite
Microcline
Molybdenite

Narsarsukite
Natrolite
Nepheline
Neptunite

Orthoclase

Pectolite
Phlogopite
Polylithionite
Pyrite
Pyrochlore
Pyrolusite
Pyrophanite
Pyrrhotite

Quartz

Ramsayite
Rhodochrosite
Riebeckite
Rinkite
Rutile

Sanidine
Serandite
Siderite
Sodalite
Sphalerite

Sphene
Synchysite

Taeniolite
Thomsonite

Vesuvianite

Willemite
Wohlerite
Wurtzite

Zircon

THE OKA COMPLEX
Aegirine
Albite
Analcite
Ancylite
Andradite
Apatite
Arfvedsonite
Augite

Barite
Biotite
Britholite

Calcite
Cancrinite
Cebollite
Chalcopyrite
Chlorite
Chrysolite

Dipside
Dolomite

Fluroite
Forsterite

Galena
Grossularite

Hauyne
Hematite
Hercynite
Hornblende

Idocrase (vesuvianite)
Ilmenite

Jarosite

Kaolinite

Labradorite
Latrappite

Magnemite

Magnesite
Magnetite
Melilite
Monazite
Monticellite
Muscovite

Natrolite
Nepheline
Niocalite

Orthoclase

Parisite
Periclase
Perovskite
Phlogopite
Pyrite
Pyrochlore
Pyrrhotite

Quartz

Richterite
Rutile

Sericite
Serpentine
Sphalerite
Sphene
Strontianite
Synchisite

Thomsonite
Titanaugite
Tremolite

Vermiculite

Wairakite
Wilkeite
Wollastonite

ORDOVICIAN FOSSILS
Corals
Billingsaria parva
Eofletcheria incerta
Brachiopods
Lingula s. 1.
Platystrophia
Dalmanella

Triolobites
Calymene
Calyplaulax
Bryozoans
Zygospira
Ostracods
Isochilina cyclindrica

PLEISTOCENE FOSSILS
FROM MONTREAL ISLAND
Softshell clam
Mya truncata
Long-neck clam
Mya arenaria
Arctic saxiclave
Hiatella arctica
Blue mussel
Mytilus edulis
Little macoma
Macoma balthica
Turban barnacle
Balanus hameri
Notched acorn barnacle
Balanus crenatus

Astarte
Astarte borealis
Freshwater clam
Lampsilis siliquoides

PLANTS

TREES

White pine
Pinus strobus
Red pine
Pinus resinosa
Pitch pine
Pinus rigida

Jack pine
Pinus banksiana
White spruce
Picea glauca
Black spruce
Picea mariana
Red spruce
Picea rubens
Eastern white cedar
Thuja occidentalis
Balsam fir
Abies balsamea
Eastern hemlock
Tsuga canadensis
Sugar maple
Acer saccharum
Red maple
Acer rubrum
Silver maple
Acer saccharinum
Basswood
Tilea americana
White ash
Fraxinus americana
Black ash
Fraxinus nigra
White elm
Ulmus americana
White oak
Quercus alba
Bur oak
Quercus macrocarpa
Red oak
Quercus rubra
Trembling aspen
Populus tremuloides
Largetooth aspen
Populus grandidentata
Balsam poplar
Populus balsamifera
Yellow birch
Betula lutea
White birch
Betula papyrifera
Beech
Fagus grandifolia
Blue beech
Carpinus caroliniana
Bitternut hickory
Carya cordiformis
Shagbark hickory
Carya ovata
Butternut
Juglans cinerea

Cottonwood
Populus deltoides
Black cherry
Prunus serotina

HORSETAILS
Scouring-rush
Equisetum hyemale
Field horsetail
Equisetum arvense
Woodland horsetail
Equisetum sylvaticum

CLUBMOSSES
Shining clubmoss
Lycopodium lucidulum
Ground-pine
Lycopodium obscurum
Ground-cedar
Lycopodium complanatum
Bristly clubmoss
Lycopodium annotinum
Running clubmoss
Lycopodium clavatum

FERNS
Rattlesnake fern
Botrychium virginianum
Cinnamon fern
Osmunda cinnamomea
Interrupted fern
Osmunda claytoniana
Royal fern
Osmunda regalis
Sensitive fern
Onoclea sensibilis
New York fern
Dryopteris novaboracensis
Leather fern
Dryopteris marginalis

Oak fern
Dryopteris disjuncta
Hay-scented fern
Dennstaedtia punctilobula
Bracken fern
Pteridum aquilinum

Maidenhair fern
Adiantum pedatum
Polypody fern
Polypodium virginianum

WATER AND SHORELINE PLANTS

Narrow-leaved cat-tail
Typha angustifolia
Broadleaved cat-tail
Typha latifolia
Bur-reed
Sparganium americanum
Branching bur-reed
Sparganium androcladum
Narrow-leaved bur-reed
Sparganium angustifolium
Green-fruited bur-reed
Sparganium chlorocarpum
Giant bur-reed
Sparganium eurycarpum
Floating bur-reed
Sparganium fluctuans
Slender bur-reed
Sparganium hyperboreum
Small bur-reed
Sparganium minimum
Northern pondweed
Potamogeton alpinus
Broad-leaved pondweed
Potamogeton amplifolius
Curly pondweed
Potamogeton crispus
Nuttal's pondweed
Potamogeton epihydrus
Shallow water pondweed
Potamogeton filiformis
Leafy pondweed
Potamogeton foliosus
Fries pondweed
Potamogeton friesii
Capillary pondweed
Potamogeton gemmiparus
Various-leaved pondweed
Potamogeton gramineus
Illinois pondweed
Potamogeton illinoensis
Floating pondweed
Potamogeton natans
Oakes pondweed
Potamogeton oakesianus

Blunt-leaved pondweed
Potamogeton obtusifolius
Sago pondweed
Potamogeton pectinalis
Clasping-leaved pondweed
Potamogeton perfoliatus
White-stemmed pondweed
Potamogeton praelongus
Small pondweed
Potamogeton pusillus
Richardson's pondweed
Potamogeton richardsonii
Robins' pondweed
Potamogeton robbinsii
Spiral pondweed
Potamogeton spirillus
Pondweed
Potamogeton vaginatus
Eel-grass pondweed
Potamogeton zosteriformis
Ditch grass
Ruppia maritima
Horned pondweed
Zannichellia palustris

Eel-grass
Zostera marina
Slender naiad
Najas flexilis
Guadaloupe naiad
Najas guadalupensis
Scheuchzeria
Scheuchzeria palustris
Seaside arrowgrass
Triglochin maritima
Marsh arrowgrass
Triglochin palustris
Water plantian
Alisma gramineum
Submerged water plantain
Alisma geyeri
Floating arrow-head
Sagittaria cuneata
Grass-leaved arrow-head
Sagittaria graminea

143

Wapato
Sagittaria latifolia

Sessile-fruiting arrow-head
Sagittaria rigida

Water weed
Eleoda canadensis

Eel-grass
Vallisneria americana

Blue-joint grass
Calamagrustis canadensis

Manna grass
Glyceria borealis

Rattlesnake grass
Glyceria canadensis

Needle spike-rush
Eleocharis acicularis

Cotton grass
*Eriophorum
 viridi-carinatum*

Water club-rush
Scirpus subterminalis

Great bulrush
Scirpus validus

Water bog-rush
Mariscus mariscoides

Sweet flag
Acorus calamus

Duckweed
Lemna minor

Ivy-leaved duckweed
Lemna trisulca

Greater duckweed
Spirodela polyrhiza

Pipewort
Eriocaulon septangulare

Pickerel-weed
Pontederia cordata

Water smartweed
Polygonum amphibium

Hornwort
Ceratophyllum demersum

Water shield
Brasenia Schreberi

Sweet white water lily
Nymphaea ordorata

Tuberous white water lily
Nymphaea tuberosa

Yellow pond lily
Nymphozanthus advena

White water crowfoot
Ranunculus aquatitlis

White water crowfoot
Ranunculus longirostris

Water cress
*Radicula nasturtium-
aquaticum*

Lake cress
Radicula aquatia

River weed
Podostemum ceratophyllum

Northern water starwort
Callitriche hermaphroditica

Vernal water starwort
Calitriche palustris

Frisch and Mey waterwort
Elatine minima

Purple loosetrife
Lythrum salicaria

Swamp loosestrife
Decodon verticillatus

Water purslane
Ludvigia palustris

Mare's tail
Hippuris vulgaris

Loose-flowered
 water-milfoil
Myriophyllum alterniflorum

Milfoil
Myriophyllum farwellii

Spiked water-milfoil
Myriophyllum exalbescens

Slender water-milfoil
Myriophyllum tenellum

Water parsnip
Sium suave

Horned bladderwort
Utricularia cornuta

Swollen-spurred
 bladderwort
Utricularia gibba

Flat-leaved bladderwort
Utricularia intermedia

Lesser bladderwort
Utricularia minor

Purple bladderwort
Utricularia purpurea

Great bladderwort
Utricularia vulgaris

Water lobelia
Lobelia dortmanna

Water marigold
Bidens beckii

Horsetail
Equisetum limosum

Braun's quillwort
Isocetes echinospora

Quillwort
Isoetes echinospora

Engelmann's quillwort
Isoetes engelmanni

Floating liverwort
Riccia fluitans

Purple fringed riccia
Ricciocarpus natans

Peat moss
Sphagnum subsecundum

Moss
Drepanocladus fluitans

Moss
Drepanocladus aduncus

Moss
Amblystegium irriguum

Moss
Hygrohypnum dilatatum

Water moss
Fantilalis antipyretica

Water moss
Fontinalis norvae-angliae

SEED PLANTS

False-melic
Schizachne purpurascens

Couch-grass
Agropyron repens

Wild-rye
Elymus innovatus

Poverty grass
Danthonia spicata

Redtop
Agrostis alba

Muhly-grass
Muhlenbergia mexicana

Nodding wood-grass
Cinna latifolia

Shorthusk
Brachyelytrum erectum

Black mountain-rice
Oryzopsis pungens

Rough mountain-rice
Orzopsis asperifolia

Woolly panic-grass
Panicum lanuginosum

Tufted bog-cotton
Eriophorum virginicum

Tawny bog-cotton
Eriophorum spissum

Bristle-stalked sedge
Carex leptalea

Three-seeded sedge
Carex trisperma

Brownish sedge
Carex brunnescens

Dewey's sedge
Carex deweyana

Pennsylvania sedge
Carex pensylvanica

Drooping wood sedge
Carex arctata

Fringed sedge
Carex crinata

Jack-in-the-pulpit
Arisaema atrorubens

Woodrush
Luzula multiflora

Death-camas
Zegadenus elegans

Little merrybells
Uvularia sessilifolia

Dogtooth violet
Erythronium americanum

Yellow clintonia
Clintonia borealis

Zigzag smilacina
Smilacina racemosa

Threeleaf smilacina
Smilacina trifolia

Starry smilacina
Smilacina stellata

Canada maianthemum
Maianthemum canadense

Rose twisted-stalk
Streptopus roseus

Downy Solomon's-seal
Polygonatum pubescens

Cucumber-root
Medeola virginiana

White trillium
Trillium grandiflorum

Painted trillium
Trillium undulatum

Purple trillium
Trillium erectum

Blue iris
Iris versicolor

Blue-eyed grass
Sisyrinchium montanum

Moccasin-flower
Cypripedium acaule

Yellow lady-slipper
Cypripedium calceolus

Oneleaf habenaria
Habenaria obtusata

Northern habenaria
Habenaria hyperborea

Small purple habenaria
Habenaria psycodes

Roundleaf habenaria
Habenaria orbiculata

Rattlesnake-plantain
Goodyera repens

Early coral-root
Corallorhiza trifida

Roundleaf orchid
Orchis rotundifolia

Sweet-fern
Uyrica asplenifolis

Sweet gale
Myrica gale

Swamp birch
Betula pumila

Beaked hazel
Corylus corylus

Green alder
Alnus crispa

Stinging nettle
Urtica procera

Wood-nettle
Laportea canadensis

Toad-flax
Comandra richardsiana

Northern comandra
Geocaulon lividum

Wild ginger
Asarum canadense

Fringed bindweed
Polygonum cilinode

Spring-beauty
Claytonia caroliniana

Marsh-marigold
Caltha palustris

Canada columbine
Aquilegia canadensis

Hooked buttercup
Ranunculus recurvatus

Kidneyleaf buttercup
Ranunculus abortivus

Wood anemone
Anemone quinquefolia

Canada anemone
Anemone canadensis

Early meadow-rue
Thalictrum dioicum

Gold-thread
Coptis groenlandica

White baneberry
Actaea pachypoda

Red baneberry
Actaea rubra

American hepatica
Hepatica americana

Blue-cohosh
Caulophyllum thalictroides

Bloodroot
Sanguinaria canadensis

Pale corydalis
Corydalis sempervirens

Pitcher-plant
Sarracenia purpurea

Roundleaf sundew
Drosera rotundifolia

Prickly gooseberry
Ribes cynosbatii

Bristly gooseberry
Ribes hirtellum

Northern gooseberry
Ribes oxyacanthoides

Bristly currant
Ribes lacustre

Skunk currant
Ribes glandulosum

American currant
Ribes americanum

Bitter currant
Ribes triste

Twoleaf miterwort
Mitella diphylla

Naked miterwort
Mitella nuda

Water-mat
Chrysosplenium americanum

Heartleaf foamflower
Tiarella cordifolia

White spiraea
Spiraea alba

Broadleaf spiraea
Spiraea latifolia

Steeple-bush
Spiraea tomentosa

Black chokeberry
Pyrus melanocarpa

Roundleaf serviceberry
Amelanchier sanguinea

Running serviceberry
Amelanchier stolonifera

Bartram's serviceberry
Amelanchier bartramiana

Barren-strawberry
Waldsteinia fragarioides

Wild strawberry
Fragaria virginiana

Woodland strawberry
Fragaria vesca

Marsh cinquefoil
Potentilla palustris

Threetooth cinquefoil
Potentilla tridentata

Dalibarda
Dalibarda repens

Yellow avens
Geum aleppicum

Cloudberry
Rubus chamaemorus

Stemless raspberry
Rubus acaulis

Dwarf raspberry
Rubus pubescens

Flowering raspberry
Rubus ordoratus

Wild red raspberry
Rubus strigosus

Black raspberry
Rubus occidentalis

Allegheny blackberry
Rubus allegheniensis

Trailing blackberry
Rubus hispidus

Canadian burnet
Sanguisorba canadensis

Meadow rose
Rosa blanda

Prickly rose
Rosa acicularis

Hedysarum
Hedysarum alpinum

American vetch
Vicia americana

Creamy peavine
Lathyrus ochroleucus

Wood sorrel
Oxalis montana

Bicknell geranium
Geranium bicknellii

Herb-Robert
Geranium robertianum

Seneca-snakeroot
Polygala senega

Fringed polygala
Polygala paucifolia

Black crowberry
Empetrum nigrum

Poison-ivy
Rhus radicans

Mountain-holly
Nemopanthus mucronata

Winterberry
Ilex verticillata

Spotted touch-me-not
Impatiens capensis

Alderleaf buckthorn
Rhamnus alnifolia

Redroot
Ceanothus americanus

Largeleaf white violet
Viola incognita

Northern white violet
Viola pallens

Kidneyleaf violet
Viola renifolia

Dog violet
Viola conspersa

Canadian violet
Viola canadensis

Smooth yellow violet
Viola pensylvanica

Downy yellow violet
Viola pubescens

Buffalo-berry
Shepherdia canadensis

Leatherwood
Dirca palustris

Fireweed
Epilobium angustifolium

Enchanter's-nightshade
Circaea alpina

Bristly aralia
Aralia hispida

Sarsaparilla
Aralia nudicaulis

Spikenard
Aralia racemosa

Sweet-cicely
Osmorhiza claytonii

Cow-parsnip
Heracleum maximum

Red-osier dogwood
Cornus stolonifera

Bunchberry
Cornus canadensis

Oneflower-pyrola
Moneses uniflora

Prince's-pine
Chimaphila umbellata

Shinleaf pyrola
Pyrola elliptica

Green pyrola
Pyrola virens

Roundleaf pyrola
Pyrola rotundifolia

One-sided pyrola
Pyrola secunda

Pinesap
Monotropa hypopithys

Indian-pipe
Monotropa uniflora

Bog laurel
Kalmia polifolia

Sheep laurel
Kalmia angustifolia

Labrador-tea
Ledum groenlandicum

Rhodora
Rhododendron canadense

Bog-rosemary
Andromeda glaucophylla

Trailing-arbutus
Epigaea repens

Leather-leaf
Chamaedaphne calyculata

Bearberry
Arctostaphylos uva-ursi

Creeping snowberry
Gaultheria hispidula

Wintergreen
Gaultheria procumbens

Black huckleberry
Gaylussacia baccata

Low-bush blueberry
Vaccinium angustifolium

Sour-top blueberry
Vaccinium myrtilloides

Blue bilberry
Vaccinium ovalifolium

Cowberry
Vaccinium vitis-idaea

Small cranberry
Vaccinium oxycoccos

Fringed loosestrife
Lysimachia ciliata

Terrestrial loosestrife
Lysimachia terrestris

Fourleaf loosestrife
Lysimachia quadrifolia

Star-flower
Trientalis borealis

Bogbean
Menyanthes trifoliata

Spurred gentian
Halenia deflexa

Northern gentian
Gentiana amarella

Spreading dogbane
*Apocynum
    androsaemifolium*

Low bindweed
Convolvulus spithamaeus

Northern hound's-tongue
Cynoglossum boreale

Tall lungwort
Mertensia paniculata

Wild mint
Mentha arvensis

American bugleweed
Lycopus americanus

Northern bugleweed
Lycopus uniflorus

Heal-all
Prunella vulgaris

Cow-wheat
Melampyrum lineare

Early pedicularis
Pedicularis canadensis

Beech-drops
Epifagus virginiana

Common plantain
Plantago major

Threeflower bedstraw
Galium triflorum

Partridge-berry
Mitchella repens

Bush-honeysuckle
Diervilla lonicera

Canada honeysuckle
Lonicera canadensis

Velvet honeysuckle
Lonicera villosa

Swamp honeysuckle
Lonicera oblongifolia

Climbing honeysuckle
Lonicera dioica

Hairy Honeysuckle
Lonicera hirsuta

Twinflower
Linnaea borealis

Squashberry
Viburnum edule

Downy viburnum
Viburnum rafinesquianum

Hobble-bush
Viburnum alnifolium

High-bush cranberry
Viburnum trilobum

Witherod viburnum
Viburnum cassinoides

Mapleleaf viburnum
Viburnum acerifolium

Canada elderberry
Sambucus canadensis

Red elderberry
Sambucus pubens

Snowberry
Symphoricarpos albus

Bluebell
Campanula rotundifolia

Marsh bell-flower
Campanula uliginosa
Gray goldenrod
Solidago nemoralis
Wrinkled goldenrod
Solidago rugosa
Largeleaf goldenrod
Solidago macrophylla
Zigzag goldenrod
Solidago flexicaulis
Hairy goldenrod
Solidago hispida
Wreath goldenrod
Solidago caesia
Bracted goldenrod
Solidago squarrosa
Graceful goldenrod
Solidago lepida
Canada goldenrod
Solidago canadensis
Grassleaf goldenrod
Solidago graminifolia
Bigleaf aster
Aster macrophyllus
Lindley's aster
Aster ciliolatus
Blue wood aster
Aster cordifolius
Acuminate aster
Aster acuminatus
Showy aster
Aster conspicuus
Flat-topped aster
Aster umbellatus
Canada pussy-toes
Antennaria canadensis
Pearly-everlasting
Anaphalis margaritacea
Ox-eye daisy
Chrysanthemum leucanthemum
Common yarrow
Achillea millefolium
Sweet petasites
Petasites palmatus
Common groundsel
Senecio vulgaris
Canada lettuce
Lactuca canadensis
White rattlesnake-root
Prenanthes alba
Tall rattlesnake-root
Prenanthes altissima

Orange hawkweed
Hieracium aurantiacum
Canada hawkweed
Hieracium canadense
Rough hawkweed
Hieracium scabrum

ANIMALS

INSECTS
Woodland cockroach
Parcoblatta pennsylvanica
Damsel fly
Agrion amatum
Clear-winged grasshopper
Camnula pellucida
Tomato hornworm
Phlegethontius quinquemaculatus
Eastern tent caterpillar
Malacosoma americanum
Graceful clear-wing sphinx moth
Hemaris gracilis
Hessian fly
Phytophaga destructor
Looper moth
Lygris serrataria
Wireworm
Agriotes isabellinus
Spruce budworm
Choristoneura fumiferana

BUTTERFLIES
Pearly eye
Lethe portlandia
Little wood satyr
Euptychia cymela
Macoun's arctic
Oeneis mocounii
Chryxus arctic
Oeneis chryxus
Jutta arctic
Oeneis jutta
Monarch
Danaus plexippus
Atlantis fritillary
Speyeria atlantis

Great spangled fritillary
Speyeria cybele
Aphrodite fritillary
Speyeria aphrodite
Bog fritillary
Boloria eunomia
Meadow fritillary
Boloria toddi
Silvery checkerspot
Melitaea mycteis
Pearl crescent
Phyciodes tharos
Tawny crescent
Phyciodes batesii
Violet tip
Polygonia interrogationis
Comma
Polygonia comma
Green Comma
Polygonia faunus
Grey comma
Polygonia progne
Hoary comma
Polygonia gracilis
Mourning cloak
Nymphalis antiopa
American tortoise shell
Nymphalis milberti
Red admiral
Vanessa cardui
American painted lady
Vanessa virginiensis
White admiral
Limenitis arthemis
Viceroy
Limenitis archippys
Coral hairstreak
Strymon titus
Grey hairstreak
Strymon melinus
Acadian hairstreak
Strymon acadica
Striped hairstreak
Strymon liparops
Early hairstreak
Erora laeta
Brown elfin
Incisalia augustinius
Hoary comma
Incisalia polios
Pine elfin
Incisalis niphon

Harvester
Feniseca tarquinius
American copper
Lycaena phlaeas
Bog copper
Lycaena epixanthe
Eastern tailed blue
Everes comyntas
Saepoilus blue
Plebeius saepolus
Silvery blue
Glaucopsyche lydamus
Spring azure
Celastrina pseudargiolus
Northern azure
Celastrina lucia
Short-tailed swallowtail
Papilio brevicauda
Tiger swallowtail
Papilio brevicauda

Tiger swallowtail
Papilio glaucus
Common sulphur
Colias philodice
Orange sulphur
Colias eurytheme
Hybrid sulphur
Colias philodice
Pink-edged sulphur
Colias interior
Little sulphur
Eurema lisa
Mustard white
Pieris napi
Cabbage white
Pieris rapae
Northern cloudy wing
Thorybes pylades
Dreamy dusky
Erynnis icelus
Juvenal's dusky wing
Erynnis juvenalis

Persius dusky wing
Erynnis persius
Arctic skipper
Carterocephalus palaemon
Least skipper
Ancyloxipha numitor
European skipper
Thymelicus lineola
Leonardus skipper
Hesperia leonardus
Laurentian skipper
Hesperia comma
Tawny-edged skipper
Polites themistocles
Peck's skipper
Polites peckius
Long dash
Polites mystic

Pocahontas skipper
Poanes hobomok

Broken dash
Wallengrenia otho
Two-spotted skipper
Atrytone bimacula
Eastern dun skipper
Atrytone ruricola
Roadside skipper
Amblyscirtes vialis
Pepper and salt skipper
Amblyscirtes hegon
Baltimore
Euphydryas phaeton
Bronze copper
Lycaena thoe
Common sooty wing
Pholisora catullus
Sleepy dusky wing
Erynnis brizo
Indian skipper
Hesperia sassacus

Smooth helical top shell
Margarites helicinus
Common atlantic chink
shell
Lacuna vincta

Common periwinkle
Littorina littorea

Smooth periwinkle
Littorina obtusata
Northern rough periwinkle
Littorina saxatis

Atlantic dogwinkle
Thais lapillus

Common northern whelk
Buccinum undatum
Salt marsh spire shell
Hydrobia minuta
Blue mussel
Mytilus edulis
Arctic wedge clam
Mesodesma arctatum
Stimpson's surf clam
Spisula polynyma

Little malcoma
Malcoma balthica
Ribbed pod shell
Siliqua costata
Long-neck clam
Mya arenaria
Soft-shell clam
Mya truncata
Common rock barnacle
Balanus balanoides
Turban barnacle
Balanus hameri
Polar starfish
Leptasterias polaris

AMPHIBIANS

Mudpuppy
*Necturus maculosus
maculosus*
Jefferson's salamander
Ambystoma jeffersonianum
Spotted salamander
Ambystoma maculatum
Red-spotted newt
*Diemictylus viridescens
viridescens*
Red-backed salamander
Plethodon cinereus cinereus
Common toad
Bufo americanus

Spring peeper
Hyla crucifer crucifer

Common tree frog
Hyla versicolor versicolor
Swamp cricket frog
Pseudacris nigrita triseriata
Bullfrog
Rana catesbeiana
Green frog
Rana clamitans
Mink frog
Rana septentrionalis

Wood frog
Rana sylvatica
Leopard frog
Rana pipiens pipiens

REPTILES

Snapping turtle
*Chelydra serpentina
serpentina*
Spotted turtle
Clemmys guttata
Eastern painted turtle
Chrysemys picta picta
Spiny soft-shelled turtle
Trionx ferox spinifera
Northern water snake
Natrix sipedon sipedon
DeKay's snake
Storeria dekayi dekayi
Red-bellied snake
*Storeria occipitomaculata
occipitomaculata*
Eastern garter snake
Thamnophis sirtalis sirtalis
Eastern ring-necked snake
*Diadophis punctatus
edwardsi*
Eastern smooth green snake
Opheodrys vernalis vernalis
Eastern milk snake
*Lampropeltis doliata
triangulum*

FISH

Sea lamprey
Petromyzon marinus

Silver lamprey
Ichthyomyzon unicuspis
Northern brook lamprey
Ichthyomyzon fossor
Lake sturgeon
Acipenser fulvescens

Atlantic sturgeon
Acipenser oxyrhynchus

Longnose gar
Lepisosteus osseus

Bowfin
Amia calva

American shad
Alosa sapidissima

Alewife
Alosa pseudoharengus

Gizzard shad
Dorosoma cepedianum

Atlantic salmon
Salmo salar

American smelt
Osmerus mordax

Mooneye
Hiodon tergisus

Central mudminnow
Umbra limi

Quillback carpsucker
Carpiodes cyprinus

White sucker
Catostomus commersoni

Longnose sucker
Catostomus catostomus

Northern redhorse
Moxostoma macrolepidotum

Silver Redhorse
Moxostoma anisurum

Greater redhorse
Moxostoma valenciennesi

Copper redhorse
Moxostoma hubbsi

River redhorse
Moxostoma carinatum

Carp
Cyprinus carpio

Fallfish
Semotilus corporalis

Fathead minnow
Pimephales promelas

Emerald shiner
Notropis atherinoides

Spottail shiner
Notropis hudsonius

Bridled shiner
Notropis bifrenatus

Spotfin shiner
Notropis spilopterus

Blackchin shiner
Notropis heterodon

Silvery minnow
Hybognathus nuchalis

Brassy minnow
Hybognathus hankinsoni

Longnose dace
Rhinichthys cataractae

Rosyface shiner
Notropis rubellus

Sand shiner
Notropis stramineus

Pugnose shiner
Notropis anogenus

Mimic shiner
Notropis volucellus

Cutlips
Exoglossum maxillingus

Yellow bullhead
Ictalurus natalis

Brown bullhead
Ictalurus nebulosus

Channel catfish
Ictalurus punctatus

Stone cat
Noturus flavus

Tadpole madtom
Noturus gyrinus

Black crappie
Pomoxis nigromaculatus

Brook silversides
Labidesthes sicculus

Freshwater drum
Aplodinotus grunniens

Capelin
Mallotus villosus

Arctic cod
Boreogadus saida

Atlantic cod
Gadus morhua

Atlantic herring
Clupea harengus

Burbot
Lota lota

Threespine stickleback
Gasterosteus aculeatus

Fourspine stickleback
Apeltes quadracus

Ninespine stickleback
Pungitius pungitius

Atlantic tomcod
Microgadus tomcod

Squirrel hake
Urophycis chuss

Marlin-spike
Nezumia bairdi

White perch
Roccus americanus

Striped bass
Roccus saxatilis

Longfin snail fish
Careproctus longipinnis

Greenland seasnail
Liparis tunicatus

American plaice
Hippoglossoides platessoides

Haddock
Melanogrammus aeglefinus

Winter flounder
Pseudopleuronectes americanus

Smooth flounder
Liopsetta putnami

American eel
Anguilla rostrata

Grass pickerel
Esox americanus

Northern pike
Esox lucius

Muskellunge
Esox masquinongy

Banded killifish
Fundulus diaphanus

Mummichog
Fundulus heteroclitus

Trout perch
Percopsis omiscomaycus

Striped bass
Roccus saxatilis

White bass
Roccus chrysops

White perch
Roccus americanus

Yellow walleye
Stizostedion vitreum

Sauger
Stizostedion canadense

Channel darter
Percina copelandi

Logperch
Percina caprodes

Sand darter
Ammocrypt pellucida

Iowa darter
Etheostoma exile

Fantail darter
Etheostoma flabellare

Smallmouth bass
Micropterus dolomieui

Rock bass
Ambloplites rupestris

Bluegill
Lepomis macrochirus

Longear sunfish
Lepomis megalotis

Pumpkinseed
Lepomis gibbosus

BIRDS

Birds which breed in St. Lawrence Valley.

Common loon
Gavia immer

Pied-billed grebe
Podilymbus podiceps

Double-crested cormorant
Phalacrocorax auritus

Great blue heron
Ardea herodias

Green heron
Butorides virescens

Black-crowned night heron
Nycticorax nycticorax

Least bittern
Ixobrychus exilis

American bittern
Botaurus lentiginosus

Mallard
Anas platyrhynchos

Black duck
Anas rubripes

Pintail
Anas acuta

Green-winged teal
Anas carolinensis

Blue-winged teal
Anas discors

American widgeon
Mareca americana

Shoveler
Spatula clypeata

Wood duck
Aix sponsa

Redhead
Aythya americana

Ring-necked duck
Aythya collaris

Common goldeneye
Bucephala clangula

Common eider
Somateria mollissima

Ruddy duck
Oxyura jamaicensis

Hooded merganser
Lophodytes cucullatus

Common merganser
Mergus merganser

Red-breasted merganser
Mergus serrator

Goshawk
Accipiter gentilis

Sharp-shinned hawk
Accipter striatus

Cooper's hawk
Accipiter cooperii

Red-tailed hawk
Buteo jamaicensis

Red-shouldered hawk
Buteo lineatus

Broad-winged hawk
Butio platypterus

Bald eagle
Haliaeetus leucocephalus

Marsh hawk
Circus cyaneus

Osprey
Pandion haliaetus

Pigeon hawk
Falco columbarius

Sparrow hawk
Falco sparverius

Spruce grouse
Canachites canadensis

Ruffed grouse
Bonasa umbellus

Ring-necked pheasant
Phasianus colchicus

Gray partridge
Perdix perdix

Virginia rail
Rallus limicola

Sora
Porzana carolina

Yellow rail
Coturnicops noveboracensis

Common galinule
Gallinula chloropus

American coot
Fulica americana

Killdeer
Charadrius vociferus

American woodcock
Philohela minor

European woodcock
Scolopax rusticola

Upland plover
Bartramia longicauda

Spotted sandpiper
Actitis macularia

Herring gull
Larus argentatus

Ring-billed gull
Larus delawarensis

Great black-backed gull
Larus marinus

Common tern
Sterna hirundo

Caspian tern
Hydroprogne caspia

Black tern
Chlidonias niger

Razorbill
Alca torda

Black guillemot
Cepphus grylle

Mourning dove
Zenaidura macroura

Yellow-billed cuckoo
Coccyzus americanus

Black-billed cuckoo
Coccyzus erythropthalmus

Barn owl
Tyto alba

Screech owl
Otus asio

Great horned owl
Bubo virginianus

Hawk-owl
Surnia ulula

Barred owl
Strix varia

Long-eared owl
Asio otus

Short-eared owl
Asio flammeus

Saw-whet owl
Aegolius acadicus

Whip-poor-will
Caprimulgus vociferus

Common nighthawk
Chordeiles minor

Chimney swift
Chaetura pelagica

Ruby-throated hummingbird
Archilochus colubris

Belted kingfisher
Megaceryle alcyon

Yellow-shafted flicker
Colaptes auratus

Pileated woodpecker
Dryocopus pileatus

Red-headed woodpecker
Melanerpes erythrocephalus
Yellow-bellied sapsucker
Sphyrapicus varius
Hairy woodpecker
Dendrocopos villosus
Downy woodpecker
Dendrocopos pubescens
Black-backed three-toed woodpecker
Picoides arcticus
Eastern kingbird
Tyrannus tyrannus
Great crested flycatcher
Myiarchus crinitus
Eastern phoebe
Sayornis phoebe
Yellow-bellied flycatcher
Empidonax flaviventris
Traill's flycatcher
Empidonax traillii
Least flycatcher
Empidonax minimus
Eastern wood pewee
Contopus virens
Olive-sided flycatcher
Nuttallornis borealis
Horned lark
Eremophila alpestris
Tree swallow
Iridoprocne bicolor
Bank swallow
Riparia riparia
Rough-winged swallow
Stelgidopteryx ruficollis
Barn swallow
Hirundo rustica
Cliff swallow
Petrochelidon pyrrhonota
Purple martin
Progne subis
Canada jay
Perisoreus canadensis

Blue jay
Cyanocitta cristata
Common raven
Corvus corax
Common crow
Corvus brachyrhynchos
Black-capped chickadee
Parus atricapillus
Boreal chickadee
Parus hudsonicus
White-breasted nuthatch
Sitta carolinensis
Red-breasted nuthatch
Sitta canadensis
Brown creeper
Certhia familiaris
House wren
Troglodytes aedon

Winter wren
Troglodytes troglodytes

Long-billed marsh wren
Telmatodytes palustris
Short-billed marsh wren
Cistothorus platensis
Catbird
Dumetella carolinensis
Brown thrasher
Toxostoma rufum
American robin
Turdus migratorius
Wood thrush
Hylocichla mustelina
Hermit thrush
Hylocichla guttata
Swainson's thrush
Hylocichla ustulata
Veery
Hylicichla fuscescens
Eastern bluebird
Sialia sialis
Golden-crowned kinglet
Regulus satrapa

Cedar waxwing
Bombycilla cedrorum

Ruby-crowned kinglet
Regulus calendula
Loggerhead shrike
Lanius ludovicianus
Common starling
Sturnus vulgaris
Yellow-throated vireo
Vireo flavifrons
Solitary vireo
Vireo solitarius
Red-eyed vireo
Vireo olivaceus
Philadelphia vireo
Vireo philadelphicus
Warbling vireo
Vireo gilvus
Black-and-white warbler
Mniotilta varia
Tennessee warbler
Vermivora peregrina
Nashville warbler
Vermivora ruficapilla
Parula warbler
Parula americana
Yellow warbler
Dendroica petechia
Magnolia warbler
Dendroica magnolia
Cape May warbler
Dendroica tigrina
Black-throated blue warbler
Dendroica caerulescens
Myrtle warbler
Dendroica coronata
Black-throated green warbler
Dendroica virens
Blackburnian warbler
Dendroica fusca
Chestnut-sided warbler
Dendroica pensylvanica

Bay-breasted warbler
Dendroica castanea
Pine warbler
Dendroica pinus
Palm warbler
Dendroica palmarum
Ovenbird
Seiurus aurocapillus
Northern waterthrush
Seiurus noveboracensis
Mourning warbler
Oporornis philadelphia
Common yellowthroat
Geothlypis trichas
Wilson's warbler
Wilsonia pusilla

Canada warbler
Wilsonia canadensis

American redstart
Setophaga ruticilla
House sparrow
Passer domesticus
Bobolink
Dolichonyx oryzivorus
Eastern meadowlark
Sturnella magna
Redwinged blackbird
Agelaius phoeniceus
Baltimore oriole
Icterus galbula
Rusty blackbird
Euphagus carolinus
Common grackle
Quiscalus quiscula
Brown-headed cowbird
Molothrus ater
Scarlet tanager
Piranga olivacea
Rose-breasted grosbeak
Pheucticus ludovicianus
Indigo bunting
Passerina cyanea

Evening grosbeak
Hesperiphona vespertina
Purple finch
Carpodacus purpureus
Pine grosbeak
Pinicola enucleator
Pine siskin
Spinus pinus
American goldfinch
Spinus tristis
Red crossbill
Loxia curvirostra
White-winged crossbill
Loxia leucoptera
Rufous-sided towhee
Pipilo erythrophthalmus
Savannah sparrow
Passerculus sandwichensis
Grasshopper sparrow
Ammodramus savannarum
Sharp-tailed sparrow
Ammospiza caudacuta
Vesper sparrow
Pooecetes gramineus
Slate-colored junco
Junco hyemalis
Chipping sparrow
Spizella passerina
Field sparrow
Spizella pusilla
White-throated sparrow
Zonotrichia albicollis
Lincoln's sparrow
Melospiza lincolnii
Swamp sparrow
Melospiza georgiana
Song sparrow
Melospiza melodia

Birds found in St. Lawrence
area but not breeding there.
Gannet
Morus bassanus

Canada Goose
Branta canadensis
Brant
Branta bernica
Snow goose
Chen caerulescens
Lesser scaup
Aythya affinis
Barrow's goldeneye
Bucephala islandica
Harlequin duck
Histrionicus histrionicus
King eider
Somateria spectabilis
White-winged scoter
Melanitta deglandi
Willow ptarmigan
Lagopus lagopus
Whimbrel
Numenius phaeopus
Solitary sandpiper
Tringa solitaria
Purple sandpiper
Erolia maritima
Least sandpiper
Erolia minutilla

MAMMALS
Common opossum
Didelphis marsupialis
Common shrew
Sorex cinereus
Smoky shrew
Sorex fumeus
Water shrew
Sorex palustris
Pygmy shew
Microsorex hoyi
Big short-tailed shrew
Blarina brevicauda
Hairy-tailed mole
Parascalops breweri
Star-nosed mole
Condylura cristata
Little brown bat
Myotis lucifugus
Eastern long-eared bat
Myotis keenii
Silver-haired bat
Lasionycteris noctivagans

Eastern pipistrellus
Pipistrellus subflavus
Big brown bat
Eptesicis fuscus
Red bat
Lasiurus borealis
Hoary bat
Lasiurus cinereus
Snowshoe hare
Lepus americanus
European hare
Lepus europaeus

Cottontail
Sylvilagus floridanus
Eastern grey squirrel
Sciurus carolinensis
Red squirrel
Tamiasciurus hudsonicus
Woodchuck
Marmota monax
Eastern chipmunk
Tamias striatus
Northern flying squirrel
Glaucomys sabrinus
Beaver
Castor canadensis
Deer mouse
Peromyscus maniculatus
White-footed mouse
Peromyscus leucopus
Bog lemming
Synaptomys cooperi
Red-backed mouse
Clethrionomys gapperi
Meadow vole
Microtus pennsylvanicus
Common muskrat
Ondatra zibethicus
Norway rat
Rattus norvegicus
House mouse
Mus musculus
Meadow jumping mouse
Zapus hudsonius

Woodland jumping mouse
Napaeozapus insignis
Porcupine
Erethizon dorsatum
Brush wolf
Canis latrans
Timber wolf
Canis lupus
Red fox
Vulpes vulpes
Gray fox
Urocyon cinereoargenteus
Black bear
Ursus americanus
Raccoon
Procyon lotor
Ermine
Mustela erminea

Long-tailed weasel
Mustela frenata
Mink
Mustela vison
Marten
Martes americana
Striped skunk
Mephitis mephitis
Otter
Lutra canadensis
Bobcat
Lynx rufus
Harbour seal
Phoca vitulina
Gray seal
Halichoerus grypus
White-tailed deer
Odocoileus virginianus
Caribou
Rangifer tarandus
White whale
Delphinapterus leucas
Pilot whale
Globicephala melaena

BIBLIOGRAPHY

GENERAL

Atlas of Canada.
Ottawa: Department of Energy, Mines and
Resources, 1957.

BARDACH, J.
Downstream: A Natural History of the River.
New York: Harper and Row, 1964.

BESTON, H.
The St. Lawrence River.
New York: Rinehart & Co., 1942.

BREDIN, T.
River of Canada.
Toronto: Longmans, 1962.

*Ice: Summary and Analysis: Eastern
Canadian Seaboard.*
Ottawa: Meteorological Branch,
Department of Transport, 1967.

JONES, J. R. E.
Fish and River Pollution.
London: Butterworths, 1964.

JUDD, W. W. and SPIERS, J. M.
A Naturalist's Guide to Ontario.
Toronto: University of Toronto Press, 1964.

KALM, P.
Travels in North America.
(Ed. A. B. Benson).
New York: Dover Publications, 1966.

LAUFF, G. H.
Estuaries.
Washington: American Association for the
Advancement of Science, Publication No. 83,
1967.

Pollution and Our Environment, (3 vols.).
Ottawa: Canadian Council of Resource
Ministers, 1966.

REID, G. K.
Ecology of Inland Waters and Estuaries.
New York: Reinhold Publishing
Corporation, 1961.

*Seismological Series of the Dominion
Observatory.*
Ottawa: Department of Mines.

St. Lawrence River Pilot.
Ottawa: Canadian Hydrographic Service,
Department of Mines, 1966.

St. Lawrence Waterway.
Canadian Geographical Journal,
November, 1955.

*St. Lawrence Waterway and Connecting
Channels.*
Ottawa: Aids to Navigation Division:
Department of Transport, 1969.

USINGER, R. L.
The Life of Rivers and Streams.
New York: McGraw-Hill Book Company,
1967.

Water Levels, 1968.
Volume 1—Inland
Volume 2—Tidal
Volume 3—Temporary Gauges
Canada Department of Energy, Mines and
Resources, 1968.

GEOLOGY

Canadian Upper Mantle Report.
Ottawa: Geological Survey of Canada,
GSC Paper 67-41.
Department of Energy, Mines and Resources,
1967.

CHAPMAN, L. J. and PUTNAM, D. F.
The Physiography of Southern Ontario.
Toronto: University of Toronto Press, 1966.

CLARK, T. H.
Guide Book.
Montreal: Geological Association of
Canada, 1963.

CLARK, T. H. and STEARN, C. W.
The Geological Evolution of North America.
New York: Ronald Press, 1960.

Continental Margins and Island Arcs.
Ottawa: Geological Survey of Canada,
Paper 66-15, Department of Mines, 1966.

GARLAND, G. D.
Continental Drift.
Toronto: University of Toronto Press, 1966.

Geology and Economic Minerals of Canada.
Ottawa: Geological Survey of Canada,
Economic Series No. 1, 1957.

FLINT, R. F.
Glacial and Pleistocene Geology.
New York: John Wiley and Sons, 1957.

JENNESS, S. E.
*Guidebook: Geology of Parts of Eastern
Ontario and Western Quebec.*
Kingston: Geological Association of Canada,
1967.

POUGH, F. H.
A Field Guide To Rocks and Minerals.
Boston: Houghton, Mifflin Co., 1960.

SABINA, A. P.
*Rocks and Minerals For The Collector:
Eastern Townships and Gaspé, Quebec.*
Ottawa: Department of Energy, Mines and
Resources, 1967.

SABINA, A. P.
Rock and Mineral Collecting in Canada
Volume II: Ontario and Quebec.
Ottawa: Department of Mines, 1965.

SHELTON, J. S.
Geology Illustrated.
San Fransisco: W. H. Freeman and
Company.

STOKES, W. L. and JUDSON, S.
Introduction to Geology.
Englewood Cliffs: Prentice-Hall, Inc., 1968.

The World Rift System.
Ottawa: Geological Survey of Canada,
Paper 66-14, Department of Mines, 1966.

PLANTS

BRUNEL, J.
Le Phytoplancton de la Baie de Chaleurs.
Montreal: Les presses de l'Universite de
Montreal, 1962.

CUNNINGHAM, G. C.
Forest Flora of Canada.
Ottawa: Queen's Printer, Bulletin 121,
Department of Northern Affairs, 1958.

DANSEREAU, P. and PAGEAU, G.
Distribution Geographique et
Ecologique du Betula Alleghaniensis.
Montreal: Memoires du Jardin
Botanique de Montreal, 1966.

DORE, W. G.
Grasses of the Ottawa District.
Ottawa: Canada Department of Agriculture,
1959.

FERNALD, M. L.
Gray's Manual of Botany.
New York: American Book Company, 1950.

FERNALD, M. L.
The Persistence of Plants in Unglaciated
Areas of Boreal America.
Memoirs of the Gray Herbarium II, 1925.

FERNALD, M. L. and KINSEY, A. C.
Edible Wild Plants of Eastern North
America.
Cornwall-on-Hudson, N.Y.: Idlewild Press,
1953.

GROVES, J. W.
Edible and Poisonous Mushrooms of
Canada.
Ottawa: Department of Agriculture, 1962.

HULTEN, E.
The Amphi-Atlantic Plants and Their
Phytogeographical Connections.
Stockholm: Almquist and Wiksell, 1958.

IRENEE-MARIE, FRERE.
Flore desmidiale de la Region de Montreal.
Laprairie, 1938.

LOUIS-MARIE, P.
Flore-Manuel de la Province de Quebec,
Canada.
Montreal: Centre de Psychologie et
Pedagogie, 1959.

MARIE-VICTORIN, FRERE.
Flore Laurentienne.
Montreal: Les Freres de Ecoles
Chretiennes, 1953.

MILES, P. M. and MILES, H. B.
Woodland Ecology.
London: Hulton Education Publications,
1968.

MONTGOMERY, F. H.
Native Wild Plants.
Toronto: The Ryerson Press, 1962.

ROWE, J. S.
Forest Regions of Canada.
Ottawa: Queen's Printer, Bull. 123,
Department of Northern Affairs, 1966.

TAYLOR, R. L. and LUDWIG, R. A.
The Evolution of Canada's Flora.
Toronto: The University of Toronto Press,
1966.

WHERRY, E. T.
The Fern Guide.
New York: Doubleday and Co., 1961.

ANIMALS

ALLEN, G. M.
Extinct and Vanishing Mammals of the
Western Hemisphere.
Lancaster, PA.: The Intelligencer Printing
Co., 1942.

BLEAKNEY, J. S.
A Zoogeographical Study of the Amphibians
and Reptiles of Eastern Canada.
Ottawa: National Museum Bulletin No. 155,
1958.

BOUSEFIELD, E. L.
Canadian Atlantic Sea Shells.
Ottawa: National Museum of Canada, 1960.

BUCHSBAUM, R.
Animals Without Backbones.
Chicago: The University of Chicago Press,
1948.

BURT, W. H.
A Field Guide to the Mammals.
Boston: Houghton Mifflin, 1952.

CAHALANE, VICTOR H.
Mammals of North America.
New York: MacMillan, 1954.

CAMERON, AUSTIN W.
Canadian Mammals.
Ottawa: Department of Northern Affairs,
1968.

CHAMBERS, E. T. D.
*The Ouananiche and Its Canadian
Environment.*
New York: Harper and Brothers, 1896.

DAY, A. M.
North American Waterfowl.
New York: Stackpole and Heck, Inc., 1949.

FROOM, B.
Ontario Snakes.
Ontario: Department of Lands and Forests,
1967.

GODFREY, W. E.
The Birds of Canada.
Ottawa: The National Museum of Canada,
1966.

HARKNESS, W. J. K. and DYMOND, J. R.
The Lake Sturgeon.
Ottawa: Ontario Department of Lands and
Forests, 1961.

KLOTS, E. B.
The New Field Book of Freshwater Life.
New York: G. P. Putnam's Sons, 1966.

LANSDOWNE, J. F. and LIVINGSTON, J. A.
Birds of the Eastern Forests: Volume 1.
Toronto: McClelland and Stewart, 1968.

LEGENDRE, V.
*Freshwater Fishes: Key to Game and
Commercial Fishes of the Province of
Quebec.*
Montreal: Universite de Montreal, 1954.

LEIM, A. H. and SCOTT, W. B.
Fishes of the Atlantic Coast of Canada.
Ottawa: Fisheries Research Board of
Canada, 1966.

LUTZ, F. E.
Field Book of Insects.
New York: G. P. Putnam's Sons, 1948.

MONTPETIT, A. N.
Poisons d'eau Douce.
Montreal: C. O. Beauchemin et Fils, 1897

HARTMAN, C. G.
Possums.
Austin: University of Texas Press, 1952.

JAQUES, H. E. and OLLIVIER, R.
How To Know The Water Birds.
Dubuque: W. C. Brown Company, 1960.

LOGIER, E. B. S.
*Frogs, Toads and Salamanders of Eastern
Canada.*
Toronto: Clarke, Irwin and Co., 1952.

PETERSON, R. L.
The Mammals of Eastern Canada.
Toronto: Oxford University Press, 1966.

PETERSON, R. T.
A Field Guide To The Birds.
Boston: Houghton, Mifflin, 1947.

SCHRENKEISEN, R.
Field Book of Freshwater Fishes.
New York: G. P. Putnam's Sons, 1963.

IMMS, A. D.
A General Textbook of Entomology.
(Revised by O. W. Richards and
R. G. Davies).
London: Methuen, 1960.

MISCELLANEOUS

HYNES, H. B. N.
The Biology of Polluted Waters.
Liverpool: Liverpool University Press, 1960.

MORGAN, ANN H.
Field Book of Ponds and Streams.
New York: Putnam's, 1930.

REID, GEORGE K.
Ecology of Inland Waters and Estuaries.
New York: Reinhold, 1961

RUTTNER, F.
Fundamentals of Limnology.
(Translated by D. G. Frey and F. E. J. Fry)
University of Toronto Press, 1963.

REGIONAL MAPS AND INFORMATION

Large-scale maps and other information
on the St. Lawrence Valley region can be
obtained at moderate cost from: Department
of Lands and Forests, Parliament Building,
Quebec City, Quebec; Quebec Department
of Natural Resources, 1620-1640
Boul. de l'Entente, Quebec 6, Quebec;
Quebec Department of Tourism, Fish and
Game, Parliament Building, Quebec City,
Quebec; Government of Canada, Department
of Energy, Mines and Resources, 601 Booth
Street, Ottawa, Ontario. A selection of film
strips and slides is available from: National
Film Board, P.O. Box 6100, Montreal 3,
Quebec.

INDEX